Current and forthcoming titles in the Bristol Classical Paperbacks series:

THE
CATULLAN
REVOLUTION

Kenneth Quinn

Second Edition
Foreword and Bibliography by Charles Martindale

BRISTOL CLASSICAL

PAPERBACKS

To Gamby

Cover illustration:
Head of an unknown girl of the time of Augustus, about 20 BC
[Paris, Louvre, cliché des Musées Nationaux]

First published in 1959 by Melbourne University Press
Revised impression 1969 published by
W. Heffer & Sons Ltd, Cambridge

Second edition published in 1999 by
Bristol Classical Press
an imprint of
Gerald Duckworth & Co. Ltd
London W1D 3JL
e-mail: inquiries@duckworth-publishers.co.uk
Website: www.ducknet.co.uk

Reprinted 2001

A catalogue record for this book is available
from the British Library

ISBN 1-85399-600-9

Printed in Great Britain by
Antony Rowe Ltd, Eastbourne

1002556829

Contents

Foreword to the 1999 Edition

We do not understand Catullus merely because he seems intelligible.[1]

The Catullan Revolution was first published in 1959, and a revised edition was issued in 1969. Thus it belongs to a decade now widely seen as one of major social and intellectual ferment in the West, culminating in the student protests in Paris that in May 1968 seemed to threaten the government of France. Quinn's elegant pamphlet – *lepidus novus libellus* indeed – was received, in Britain at least, in a manner that was generally lukewarm or hostile.[2] When I went to Oxford in 1968 it was one of the few books that seemed to me to offer a future of bright promise for the study of Latin literature – another was Steele Commager's *The Odes of Horace* – but caution was enjoined by our tutors. I by contrast agreed with the sentiments of the Cambridge literary critic H.A. Mason: 'It is, so far as I know, a law without important exceptions, that the majority of the world's classical scholars are not *Kulturträger*; they do not transmit to us the greatness of the great works they study'.[3] Today it perhaps takes an exercise of the historical imagination to see why the work, a milestone in Catullan[4] studies, appeared threatening to some, a beacon of light to others.

On the first page Quinn tells us what to his view was 'the most important task: to understand, and judge, the work of art itself from the data it itself furnishes and constitutes'. To achieve this in a fully effective way classicists needed to approach ancient poetry with the same tools and in the same way as contemporary critics of English literature. Of particular importance here were the writings of T.S. Eliot, quoted on a number of occasions by Quinn, and F.R. Leavis, who is thanked in the Preface and who claimed that what above all he learned from Eliot's 1920 collection *The Sacred Wood* was 'the principle (as Mr Eliot himself states it) that "when you judge poetry it is as poetry you must judge it and not as another thing"'.[5] The approach of these writers and others (in particular I.A. Richards and William Empson) was fostered and institutionalised in universities and schools particularly as a result of the efforts of a group of American critics, including Cleanth Brooks (whose influential *The Well-Wrought Urn: Studies in the Structure of Poetry* was published in 1947), John Crowe Ransom, and others. The now not-so-new New Criticism became a kind of hegemonic pedagogic practice, and, though it has become the target for newer forms of criticism, its effects continue to be felt today. The focus of attention was the individual poem, conceived as an elaborate verbal structure, rather than matters biographical, historical, or ideological; 'the words on the page', text not context. New Critics tended to prefer short poems, best adapted to their style of attentive 'close reading'. Eliot admired writers who, on his reading of them, were marked by poise, balance, and lack of commitment to party-politics (in particular 'left-wing' or 'radical' politics). In his essay on the poet Andrew Marvell (1921), whom he describes as 'a lukewarm partisan', he offers his famous definition of wit as something that 'involves, probably, a recognition, implicit in the expression of every experience, of other kinds of experience which are possible'; and he observes that 'this alliance of levity and seriousness (by which the seriousness is intensified)' is a mark of poetry which is mature and civilised.[6] The American New Critics, originally mostly southern conservatives, had similar preferences, stressing the importance for poetry of ambiguity and its attendant tropes, irony and paradox. Unlike science, poetry, for Brooks, does not make statements, but enacts, like a play, 'a pattern of resolved stresses'.[7] In consequence a poem's 'real meaning' cannot be paraphrased. The unity of a poem is not 'logical' but 'poetic', and lies in 'the unification of attitudes into a hierarchy subordinated to a total and governing attitude'. Scientific terms are 'pure denotations', but the poet – and here Brooks quotes Eliot – has to 'dislocate language into meaning', and 'his task is finally to unify experience' by 'the assertion of the union of opposites'.[8] Leavis and his followers also stressed the link between poetry and the rhythms of actual speech. So Milton is condemned for writing which is 'incanta-tory, remote from speech', whereas 'it should be plain...that subtlety of movement in English verse depends upon the play of the natural sense movement and intonation against the verse structure, and that "natural", here, involves a reference, more or less direct, to idiomatic speech'.[9] The aim is for 'sharp, concrete realization' and 'sensuous particularity', qualities that Leavis found missing in Milton's later work. It is easy to see how such a taste could lead to an enthusiasm for Catullus. Thus Quinn's Catullus is commended, in Leavisite fashion, for 'directness of speech' and for 'colloquialism', as well as for his ability to reduce 'difficult or novel thought to effective and communicable form' (pp. 59 and 71). Thereby he is reinscribed into the system of rewards and punishments meted out by the dominant schools of advanced literary criticism.

The diffusion of the New Criticism is one of the great success stories of the twentieth-century academy, and it brought into being, throughout the Anglo-Saxon world, a manner of talking in detail about poetic texts which was very different from the modes of criticism common in earlier centuries;[10] above all it privileged *literary criticism* in a way that some of us, amid the present dominance of new historicisms and culturalisms, can still find, in certain ways, exemplary for our own practice. New Criticism is frequently taken to task for formalism (the concentration on poetic forms to the neglect of the ideological formations which on other views give them their meaning), and certainly draws a sharp – and of course contestable – distinction between poetic and non-poetic modes of discourse, in that respect resembling other early twentieth-century formalisms. But the New Critics themselves would have resisted the charge of formalism, arguing, as had the critics of the Romantic period before them, that in great literature, to a unique degree, form and content are one. In due course, after a customary time-lag, classicists began to follow the New Critical lead, and the best of this criticism still wears, to my mind, surprisingly well. Among early examples were Niall Rudd, 'Colonia and her Bridge: A Note on the Structure of Catullus 17' (1959);[11] Commager's *The Odes of Horace* (1962);

Adam Parry's 'The Two Voices of Virgil's *Aeneid*', first published in *Arion* in 1963, which set the terms for the subsequent debate about the poem that is still with us; David West's *The Imagery and Poetry of Lucretius* (1969); and, on a much more massive scale, Gordon Williams' *Tradition and Originality in Roman Poetry* of 1968. *The Catullan Revolution*, then, was part of an important trend. The New Criticism successfully colonised the whole field of Latin poetry, perhaps because Latinists find it easy to reconcile with their traditional philological formalistic concerns. A new account of Catullus as compelling as Quinn's would need to take cognisance of literary-critical and theoretical developments which began, in other disciplines, during the later 1960s and which have questioned many of the founding assumptions of the New Critical paradigm.

According to Quinn's Preface his book 'deals mainly with literary criticism'. Certainly it is a manifesto for a particular kind of poetry and a particular way of writing about it, and as such it can be considered a *critical* project. But it contains relatively few close readings, and none that are as detailed or as subtle as the examples listed above.[12] Superficially it appears more a work of literary history, if one of a strongly evaluative stamp.[13] Quinn argues for a 'revolution' in Roman poetic practice led by Catullus, who belonged to a school, or at any rate a loose grouping, of writers with shared or overlapping interests and concerns whom we term the 'New Poets' or Neoterics.[14] Catullus in this account is both typical of the new poetry and its most effective practitioner (since only tiny fragments of the others survive, this can only be a guess). It is not long before a subtext begins to show: 'The poetry he [Catullus] wrote is close in form, style and spirit to much of our own contemporary poetry and, like our own poetry, it differs sharply in form, style and spirit from the poetry it largely superseded. It is this up-to-dateness that makes Catullus popular with us and causes us to regard him as important' (p. 3). Catullus, in other words, is to play the same role as Eliot and other modernists, and the revolution turns out to be yet another eternal return of the crisis of modernism: 'the nature of the phenomenon with which we have to deal...can be more readily understood, therefore, today than fifty years ago as a result of the comparable renewal that we have seen in the language of poetry in our own literature' (p. 59). The word 'revolution' also suggests excitement, mould-breaking, youth, sexual freedom, the whole liberated world that was to climax in *les événements* in Paris in 1968, summed up in Larkin's famous words from his poem 'Annus Mirabilis' (*High Windows*, 1974):

> Sexual intercourse began
> In nineteen sixty-three
> (Which was rather late for me) --
> Between the end of the *Chatterly* ban
> And the Beatles' first LP.

Quinn might have been influenced by the title of Sir Ronald Syme's seminal work *The Roman Revolution* (1939), which charts the rise to power of the Emperor Augustus. The intertextuality could be read as encoding a hostility to 'the establishment' and to Augustan Roman values and their supposed modern equivalents.[15]

The story that Quinn tells has become normative. Catullus and his friends might well be delighted by it; as new poets eternally, they remain forever new, forever young. To ask 'Was there really a Catullan Revolution?' is, however, to frame the question in too positivistic a fashion. What Quinn's story shows is how any piece of literary history depends on being troped in a particular way, and how the manner of its telling reflects modern concerns and debates. You can describe Catullus' poetry in such a way as to foreground the continuities with the past ('tradition'), or to stress the breaks ('revolution', 'new poetry') – neither account is more 'historical' than the other. Shorn of its provocations and smoothed into judiciousness, a similar story to Quinn's appears in many standard works of reference, for example Conte's magisterial *Latin Literature*, where it assumes the form of sober 'history'. Neoteric taste, Conte opines, 'marks a decisive turn in the history of Latin literature.'[16] 'It is a revolution in literary taste but also a revolution in ethics.' Like Quinn, and similarly undeterred by the unusually lacunose nature of the material, Conte has no problems about distinguishing Catullan profundities from the lesser achievements of his predecessors: the preciosities of Laevius (a poet of the previous generation whose exuberantly experimental writing survives only in fragments) or 'the often mannered elegance and the artificial experiments with the Greek models on the part of Lutatius Catulus's circle'. This last is a reference to a small group of erotic epigrams from the second century BC which, from a different perspective, could easily be redescribed as very 'like' some of Catullus'. Indeed Aulus Gellius, an admirer of Catullus who preserves them for us, comments that 'nothing neater, more charming (*venustius*), more polished, or more refined (*tersius*) can be found in Greek or Latin' (19.9) – *venustus* is for Catullus himself a term of high critical praise. Both Quinn and Conte in other words are determined to emplot their material into a narrative of radical change. But with Quinn, as with Catullus, issues then current about how to write and how to live give the whole argument urgency and point. In Conte energetic troping has congealed wholly into academic history.

The Catullan Revolution, then, can be seen as a text for the 1960s. That, of course, does not diminish its interest or authority for us. All readings of past texts entail a negotiation with present concerns to create what the philosopher and hermeneuticist Hans-Georg Gadamer called a 'fusion of horizons' between text and reader. One result is that texts are continually re-interpreted, and authors continually re-invented, through the centuries of their reception.[17] That does not mean that earlier readings simply go out of date; rather we can engage in a productive dialogue with them in the formation of our own readings, particularly so in the case of those, like Quinn's, that are compellingly imagined and powerfully presented. In the case of Catullus the varieties of re-interpretations and re-inventions seem unusually diverse, even troublingly so. Part of the reason may lie in the variety of the poet's output, lacking a clear 'centre'. Two images of Catullus have predominated in our century: Catullus as a peculiarly accessible and 'modern' lyrical poet of intense personal feeling; and Catullus the heir of Alexandria and Callimachus, and

precursor of the elegists for whom he was *doctus Catullus*.[18] Some
have felt that there was a tension between the two images (and
even that there were two Catulluses), others, including Quinn,
have sought to reconcile them as part of a consistent aesthetic,
the so-called 'New Poetics'. But there was a very different Catul-
lus among a number of ancient readers, a Catullus who is
essentially an epigrammatist, a writer of light verse, much of it
scabrous and priapic in character. This is the Catullus whom
Quintilian (10.1.96) presented as a master of *acerbitas*, to whom
alone Martial saw himself as second (*uno sed tibi sim minor
Catullo*, 10.78.16), whom the younger Pliny imitated for relaxa-
tion. Pliny describes the poems of a friend modelled on Catullus
and Calvus (another leading neoteric) thus: *quantum illis leporis,
dulcedinis, amaritudinis, amoris*, 'how much they have of charm,
sweetness, bitterness, love' (1.16). Interestingly the Loeb trans-
lates *amoris* as 'tender passion', but more plausibly it simply
refers to erotic poems, just as *amaritudinis* refers to invectives.
Pliny experimented himself in 'hendecasyllabic' verse of this
kind: *iocamur, ludimus, amamus, dolemus, querimur, irascimur*,
'I joke, play, love, grieve, complain, grow angry' (4.14). Some of
the verses are 'slightly risqué', *petulantiora*, but that for Pliny is
quite in accordance with the best Roman tradition – thus he
delights his leisure hours (*oblectamus otium temporis*). In similar
vein his friend Augurinus in playful verse referred to *meus
Catullus*, and associated Catullus' name with Pliny's (*Letters*
4.27). Critics of a historicist bent might reflect, perhaps with
dismay, that this is the Catullus for whom there is the most
extensive ancient 'evidence', and who for such critics might thus
have to be the 'real' Catullus (recently J.K. Newman has argued,
on historicist lines, that Catullus should be seen primarily as a
satirist). It was essentially the Catullus of Martial who was taken
up by a number of poets in Renaissance Italy, including the great
Pontano; for them Catullus was *lascivus, mollis, tener*, and *doctus*,
a poet of wit, ebullience, and *joie de vivre*, a poet in love with
poetry and his fellow poets, an ideal model for a humanist coterie,
but not a poet of grand passions.[19]

The Renaissance had identified Catullus' Lesbia with Clodia, notorious sister of the radical politician Clodius and wife of the *nobilis* Metellus Celer, consul in 60 BC.[20] Nineteenth-century scholarship attempted a much fuller account of Catullus' life based on the same assumption – the crucial work was Ludwig Swabe's *Quaestiones Catullianae* of 1862 – and this encouraged biographical readings of the poems (something similar happened with Shakespeare's Sonnets at about the same time). The Victorian artists Alma-Tadema and Poynter both painted pictures of Lesbia with or without her poet-lover. But it was the twentieth, not the nineteenth century, that was to be the century of Catullus and Lesbia. For Tennyson it was Catullus' love for his brother that was the more important, and he echoed the famous lines from poem 101 in *In Memoriam* 57:

> I hear it now, and o'er and o'er,
>   Eternal greetings to the dead;
>   And 'Ave, Ave, Ave,' said,
> 'Adieu, adieu' for evermore.

A lighter poem of 1883, 'Frater Ave atque Vale' picks up the same phrase to constitute a touchingly elegant tribute:

> Row us out from Desenzano, to your Sirmione row!
> So they rowed, and there we landed – 'O venusta Sirmio!'
> There to me through all the groves of olive in the summer
>   glow,
> There beneath the Roman ruin where the purple flowers
>   grow,
> Came that 'Ave atque Vale' of the Poet's hopeless woe,
> Tenderest of Roman poets nineteen-hundred years ago,
> 'Frater Ave atque Vale' – as we wandered to and fro
> Gazing at the Lydian laughter of the Garda Lake below,
> Sweet Catullus' all-but-island, olive-silvery Sirmio!

The metre deftly evokes the world of Catullus' *versiculi*,[21] in particular poem 31 on Sirmio – it is on the peninsula that Tennyson feels the presence of the poet (in reality the Roman ruin is of imperial date). For Swinburne also brotherly love was more important than love for Lesbia, and in his poem 'To Catullus' (1883) Swinburne brings Catullus into a homosocial fellowship of poet-brothers across the centuries:[22]

> To thee was Caesar's self nor dear nor dread
> Song and the sea were sweeter than each other:
> How should I living fear to call thee dead,
>   My brother?

For both writers – as for Aubrey Beardsley who translated poem 101 for the 'decadent' journal *The Savoy* in 1896 – Catullus was a poet who could easily be accommodated to a world of Aestheticism, Art for Art's Sake, and poetic 'purity' (Swinburne associated him with Baudelaire).[23] Much later Yeats in his Preface to *The Oxford Book of Modern Verse* (1939) cites Catullus as one who had been a model for pure poetry for his generation. So too for Quinn, disciple of Eliot and Modernism, Catullus' is 'the poetry of *littérature pure*' (p. 68).

Unsurprisingly these very different images of Catullus lead to very different readings of individual poems. A prime example is poem 8 (for the text and Quinn's account of it, see pp. 92-5). This poem apparently always reduced Macaulay to tears, and it is often read as a *cri de coeur*, an anguished outpouring following a serious breach with Lesbia (though in fact the *puella* is not named). However, some would see it rather as a humorous presentation of Catullus as a jilted lover from Comedy.[24] It is one of the virtues of *The Catullan Revolution* that it stresses the *Romanness* of Catullus' poetry and its background in Latin literature, whereas others foreground the Greek and Alexandrian elements. Callimachus may have been a more glamorous figure for Catullus to cite than Plautus or other early Roman poets, but that that does not mean that he is a more potent presence. Certainly the tropes of Catullus 8 are easy enough to parallel in Roman comedy. The question of tone cannot easily be settled by close analysis, and is likely to depend on one's view of wider issues. The poem is indeed like a dramatic *scena*, but without a clear dramatic context (unless we supply one from Catullus' 'life'). In the work of the elegists it is easy to construct an implied author who is not quite the same as the character in the poems, even if he bears the same name, and this opens a gap both for an effect of subjectivity and for interpretation. By contrast poem 8 reads more 'objectively' as a mimesis of the thoughts of a jealous lover. It is perhaps this which has led critics to believe in Catullus' 'sincerity'. As Veyne puts it, 'Catullus has the sincerity of classical theater', and he quips 'it is Catullus's *art* that is sincere'. Veyne compares the effect to that of a modern pop song; in his view in poem 8 'the Jealous Man is on stage'.[25] Another possible response would be to say that Catullus has not succeeded in making all his poems fully public property – we seem to be reading texts that do not provide us with enough material to interpret them satisfactorily; hence perhaps the disconcerting divergence of irreconcilable interpretations.

How important a poet is Catullus? And how can a sense of his particular greatness be made available to readers today? It is a great merit of Quinn's book that it does not shirk such questions of evaluation. Quinn's principal claim is that Catullus' greatness depends on his invention of a new sort of short lyrical poem that anticipates the meditative mode of modern lyric as described by Eliot, which has freed itself from dependence on a particular context of reception, more an argument by the poet with herself than an address to the public.[26] That could help to explain why Catullus has been such a modern favourite.[27] In Britain it is only in this century that he has become one of the four or five most valued Latin authors. In the Middle Ages Catullus' work was lost, save for one of the wedding songs which was anthologised. Indeed only a single manuscript, fraught with textual corruption, survived into the Renaissance. As Jowett in Tom Stoppard's play about A.E. Housman, *The Invention of Love*, colourfully puts it:

> ...anyone with a secretary knows that what Catullus really wrote was already corrupt by the time it was copied twice, which was about the time of the first

Roman invasion of Britain: and the earliest copy that has come down to *us* was written about 1,500 years after that. Think of all those secretaries! – corruption breeding corruption from papyrus to papyrus, and from the last disintegrating scrolls to the first new-fangled parchment books, with a thousand years of copying still to come, running the gauntlet of changing forms of script and spelling, and absence of punctuation – not to mention mildew and rats and fire and flood and Christian disapproval to the brink of extinction as what Catullus really wrote passed from scribe to scribe, this one drunk, that one sleepy, another without scruple, and of those sober, wide-awake and scrupulous, some ignorant of Latin and some, even worse, fancying themselves better Latinists than Catullus – until! – finally and at long last – mangled and tattered like a dog that has fought its way home, there falls across the threshold of the Italian Renaissance the sole surviving witness to thirty generations of carelessness and stupidity: the *Verona Codex* of Catullus; which was almost immediately lost again, but not before being copied with one last opportunity for error. And there you have the foundation of the poems of Catullus as they went to the printer for the first time, in Venice 400 years ago.[28]

Catullus was admired in Southern Europe from the sixteenth century onwards but was less popular in Britain, partly perhaps because of the more conservative nature of English humanism (as we have seen, he was not in the medieval canon); only one edition of his works was published in England before 1700. He was not an important feature of the school curriculum; at St Paul's, for example, in 1580 the list of authors approved for study comprised Terence, Cicero, Caesar, Sallust, Virgil, Horace, Ovid, Valerius Maximus, Seneca, Persius, the younger Pliny, Juvenal, Quintilian, Silius Italicus – no Catullus, Lucretius, or Propertius – and similar lists exist for many other schools.[29] Catullus' presence in English poetry is also relatively limited, in comparison with, say, Ovid's. No great English poet sought to become the English Catullus, as Jonson and Pope became the English Horace or Milton the English Virgil. Only a small number of poems were regularly translated and imitated, above all, the sparrow poems, the kiss poems, the marriage songs (basis of Spenser's great *Epithalamion*) – other popular poems have been 8, 45 ('Acme and Septimius', charmingly Englished by Cowley), 63 (the 'Attis', a nineteenth-century favourite for its wildness and sublimity), 70 (seemingly the first of Catullus' poems to be translated, by Sidney), 72, 75, 85, 92, and 101. Catullus thus partially fails one test by which one can judge whether an ancient poet is fully alive in the later culture.

Quinn clearly does not think that all Catullus' poems are of equal value. To make distinctions among them he introduces the notion of 'levels of intent', that is 'differing degrees of devotion to the task of making poetry, varying...from the most casual versifying to the most complete surrender to inspiration' (p. 32). This idea has not in general found favour,[30] but one can see why Quinn has resort to it. Take poem 49, addressed to Cicero:

> Disertissime Romuli nepotum,
> quot sunt quotque fuere, Marce Tulle,
> quotque post aliis erunt in annis,
> gratias tibi maximas Catullus
> agit pessimus omnium poeta,
> tanto pessimus omnium poeta
> quanto tu optimus omnium patronus.

> (Most eloquent of the descendants of Romulus, as many as there are or were, Marcus Tullius, or shall be afterwards in other years, Catullus, worst poet of all, gives you greatest thanks, as much the worst poet of all as you are the best advocate of all.)

This is another poem, which, deprived of a context, seems hardly interpretable. Some give it point by inventing a context (for example Catullus is thanking Cicero ruefully for his successful defence of Caelius from the accusations of Clodia). Critics disagree about whether the poem is ironic (can *omnium* be taken with *patronus* rather than with *optimus?*), or straighforwardly eulogistic. Others (inevitably) try to resolve that issue by arguing that the contextlessness or undecidability is precisely the poem's point.[31] But on any of these readings it seems a slight enough piece of writing.

Contrast this with a much more admired piece, the first of the two kiss poems, number 5. This belongs to a type of poem that Horace was later to make his own and which has consequently become identified by a phrase of his, *carpe diem* – since we all die, let us enjoy life while we may (a familiar example in English is Marvell's 'To His Coy Mistress'). Catullus contrasts himself and Lesbia with the old men we so often meet in comedy and calls for kisses without end.[32] Elegantly and prettily as this is done, I see little of greatness here. Only lines 3-5 seem to me to rise to excellence:

> soles occidere et redire possunt,
> nobis, cum semel occidit brevis lux,
> nox est perpetua una dormienda.

The sentiments are the commonest of commonplaces, but the expression makes of them what many would call a 'classic' statement. The effect, simultaneously graceful and solemn, lies partly in the way the weight of feeling cuts against the metrical lightness (though a couple of elisions slow down the verse). The powerful, semi-rhyming monosyllables *lux* and *nox* are placed in sharp antithesis at the end and beginning of successive lines; *nox* (used of a date with a lover, here a date with death) is balanced by the heavy gerundive *dormienda*. The quality of what Catullus has achieved here might be contrasted with the (comparative) failure of his finest translators. Campion goes for too much weight:

> Heaven's great lamps do dive
> Into their west, and straight again revive.

But soon as once set is our little light,
Then must we sleep one ever-during night.

Jonson for too much lightness:

Suns that set may rise again,
But if once we lose this light,
'Tis, with us, perpetual night.[33]

The idea of 'levels of intent' might suggest that at such moments
Catullus is aiming higher than in the poem for Cicero.

The raising of Catullus' status in our century is often linked
with the claim that he is a great love poet.[34] Thus for Conte, as
for many others, love is the centre of Catullus' world, 'the central
emotion of life, its essence and raison d'être'.[35] Some critics have
found poem 72, one of a number in which Catullus inscribes his
sexual feelings into a discourse of *amicitia*, confused and confus-
ing in expression. By contrast Mason sees its greatness as deriving
from its fully adequate instantiation of a great insight about love:

> If you suppose that Catullus cared about mutuality and
> wanted to go on feeling that his *amor* was sanctioned in
> the way family bonds seemed to him to be sanctioned,
> then you might suppose that the horror of *impensius uror*
> was not that while he found he could detach his mind
> from Lesbia he could not do the same for his penis, but
> that he loved her more than ever in every sense the word
> had for him while knowing that the emergent structure of
> liking and respect was permanently ruined. Such a condi-
> tion seems to me of fathomless depth so long as we suppose
> Catullus to have a vast notion of what loving was.[36]

Mason's analysis has the merit of explaining why Catullus' poem
might matter to us (the concentration of 'complex sexual feeling'
which we might share into 'short and simple expressions'), but
of course it rests on the assumption of a shared human nature in
the experience of sexual love. As such it is vulnerable to the critics

of this kind of universalism or 'essentialism': both historicists who deny that Catullus' *amor* is the same as our 'love', and feminists, who resist the viewpoint of the *male* universal subject. Certainly Mason does not consider the possibility that Catullus' poems, which regularly figure Lesbia as whore and goddess, might be considered misogynistic. Poems that are expressions of the agonies of the bruised male ego or constructions of women as objects of erotic fantasy might not necessarily chime with the experience of love by women. At all events we need rigorously feminist readings of Catullus' poems to explain how they might be valued from perspectives of alterity.[37]

* * * * *

A substantial amount of work has been done on Catullus, obviously, since 1959 (some of the best in English is given in the bibliography). Readings of poems or groups of poems abound, mostly still conducted according to a New Critical paradigm, though sometimes with a deconstructionist gloss (a good example would be Denis Feeney's attractive account of poem 68). But, as William Batstone notes, 'in recent years no general interpretation or reinterpretation of Catullus has emerged which one would call standard or authoritative. In fact, no general interpretation has emerged in recent years despite the work of the past two decades'.[38] For that reason alone *The Catullan Revolution* still commands respect. The focus of recent scholarship includes the following:

1. *Historical context.* Historicists believe that the more we know about the historical 'background' from which Catullus' poems emerged, the better we will understand them (Quinn, of course, would disagree). Perhaps the most interesting work of this kind has come from Peter Wiseman. Wiseman has advanced a number of bold if unprovable hypotheses – that Lesbia is not Clodia Metelli, that Catullus should be identified with the mime-writer of that name mentioned in some ancient *testimonia*, that some of the poems (for example the hymn no. 34) may have been written for performance – but in the final estimate how

much does all this do to alter our overall sense of the poetry? The issue of text and context remains, and will remain, a concern of all students of literature. Historicists New and old are currently in the ascendant in Classics, so revisiting Quinn's book might assist in promoting a much-needed aesthetic turn.

2. *Callimacheanism.* A vast, perhaps an excessive, amount of work has been done on the influence of Callimachus and other Alexandrian writers, which has been a principal concern of Latinists for decades (typically this is the longest section of this necessarily somewhat jejune mini-survey, so much are we all the children of our time). W.V. Clausen argued that the Revolution began when the captured Greek writer Parthenius came to Rome. The Alexandrianising approach works best with some of the longer poems, in particular 64, Catullus' avant-garde mini-epic, and 68, his most complex elegy. *The Catullan Revolution* had little to say about these works, and indeed Quinn dismisses 68 – which arguably more than any other poem bears the full weight of Catullus' poetic personality and therefore reveals most of his special 'virtue' (to use a term of Walter Pater) – as 'rather unsatisfactory' (p. 83). The stress on Callimachus chimes with a pre-occupation with poetic reflexivity (another late legacy of the New Criticism, which shades into the concerns of post-structuralism). Poem 64, for example, is easy to read as a poem about art, which we might see as figured in the labyrinth through which Ariadne guides Theseus with a fine thread, *tenui filo* (113). This image, along with the poem's numerous metaphors of constructing, threading, interweaving, might imply a commitment to stylistic *tenuitas.* Ariadne's thread, then, could be read as a symbol of poetic praxis in general and of poem 64, with its narrative weavings, windings and interlacements, in particular. A laby-rinth is a piece of ambiguous figuring, since it can represent order under chaos, planned chaos, or chaos simply; art so figured can bring entrapment and confusion, or a complex clarity.[39] So the elaborate narrative structure of 64, together with repeated words and images, both encourages and resists a unified reading. Are the recurrences part of a grand unity, or are there, as Derrideans

insist, only differences? The emphasis on Callimacheanism has often led to a neglect of Roman elements in Catullus.[40] J.K. Newman argues that Catullus' debt to Alexandria has been exaggerated. He sees in the satiric, histrionic, carnivalesque character of iambography 'a single rubric...that will unite all his poetic achievement, instead of requiring us to discount and discredit the part that will not fit'.[41] But Newman has trouble integrating the longer poems into his account, and a balanced synthesis is still needed.

3. *Obscenity*. C.J. Fordyce in his edition of 1961 notoriously omitted 'a few poems that do not lend themselves to comment in English'. In fact those poems were 32 in number. Obscenity is an important part of Catullus' *oeuvre*, and from the 1960s again a part of its appeal for some, part of its supposed 'modernity'. Any adequate account of Catullus must come to terms with this element in his poetry, about which Quinn had little to say. Progress has been made in investigating obscene terminology (in particular by J.N. Adams in *The Latin Sexual Vocabulary*), while Amy Richlin's *The Garden of Priapus* has also been rightly influential.[42] A broader theoretical framework would bring increased insights.

4. *Sexuality and gender*. This is another area where much important work has recently been done, though more in connection with the elegists than with Catullus. The approach has tended to be historical and sociological rather than psychoanalytic. An important exception is Micaela Janan's *When The Lamp is Shattered*, which usefully applies a Lacanian analysis to the poems. Janan connects a readerly desire for a unity in the Catullan corpus (achieved, for example, by an autobiographical approach) with the Lacanian subject's sense of loss and search for an elusive wholeness. There has also been a stress on the textuality necessarily involved in experiences of sex and gender. In Catullus 35, for example, we find the standard cast of Roman love poetry, the poet-lover who writes poetry in the modern style and his mistress, a *docta puella*. The poem acknowledges its textuality in its address

to the papyrus page on which it is written. *Tenero* (1) shows that
Caecilius is a love poet, and he is writing a poem, evidently in
an Alexandrianising manner, on the *Magna Mater* (compare
Catullus 63). What makes the *puella,* who is *Sapphica...Musa
doctior* 'more learned than Sappho's Muse', love Caecilius is her
taste for his poetry. Sex and text are elided. As Veyne puts it 'To
love is to write and to be loved, to be read'.[43] The matter is
clinched by *venuste* in 16 describing the way Caecilius' poem is
composed. *Venustus* ('sexy') appears to be a vogue word for
Catullus that applies to everything he approves in poetry, life and
manners; it connects, of course, with Venus, goddess of sex.

* * * * * *

My view, unlike Quinn's, is that, in the end, Catullus is not one
of the world's greatest poets (though I would happily be per-
suaded otherwise). Unlike Virgil, Horace, or Ovid, he seemed –
at least on the evidence that we have – unable to forge a coherent
body of work, though this very inability, which produces drafts
and fragments of the self, can also be regarded as a source of a
certain strength.[44] His shorter poems are, arguably, over rated, in
comparison with, say, Horace's *Odes.* However, I do not want to
end this foreword on a negative note but instead with a poem
that does, to my thinking, attain excellence, number 11:

> Furi et Aureli, comites Catulli,
> sive in extremos penetrabit Indos,
> litus ut longe resonante Eoa
>   tunditur unda,
> sive in Hyrcanos Arabasve molles
> seu Sacas sagitteriferosve Parthos,
> sive quae septemgeminus colorat
>   aequora Nilus,
> sive trans altas gradietur Alpes,
> Caesaris visens monimenta magni,
> Gallicum Rhenum, horribiles quoque ulti-
>   mosque Britannos,
> omnia haec, quaecumque feret voluntas

caelitum, temptare simul parati,
pauca nuntiate meae puellae
  non bona dicta:
cum suis vivat valeatque moechis,
quos simul complexa tenet trecentos,
nullum amans vere, sed identidem omnium
  ilia rumpens;
nec meum respectet, ut ante, amorem,
qui illius culpa cecidit veluti prati
ultimi flos, praetereunte postquam
  tactus aratro est.

(Furius and Aurelius, comrades of Catullus, whether he penetrates to the farthest Indians, where the shore is pounded by the far-echoing eastern wave, or to the Hyrcanians and the arrow-bearing Parthians, or the levels which the sevenfold Nile colours, or whether he goes beyond the high Alps, visiting the monuments of mighty Caesar, the Gallic Rhine, the horrible and furthest Britons too, ready together to attempt whatever the will of the heavenly ones brings, give as brief message to my girl these not fair words: farewell and long life with her adulterers, whom she holds in her embrace three hundred together, loving none truly, but again and again bursting the belly's arteries of all; and let her not look to my love, as before, which, by her fault, has fallen, like the flower at the meadow's edge, after it has been touched by a passing plough.)

Catullus has responded well to the protocols of reading spread by the New Criticism, a mode of criticism with which I myself was brought up; so I offer a reading in this tradition as a homage to Kenneth Quinn and those others who helped Latinists to see the value of this approach for their own work. 'Catullus 11 is a complex poem which anticipates Horace's *Odes*, it can be argued, in the use of contrasted registers and tones, the contrived structural asymmetry, the unexpected turns in the argument, the plangent dying fall. Catullus sometimes treats his affair as a kind of marriage, and this poem perhaps makes the renunciation of love into a formal divorce, one form of which was a *repudium per litteras* (cf. *nuntiate* and *moechis*).[45] The opening stanzas are easily read as a humorous, hyperbolical, and ebullient tribute to his friends, or seeming friends, since a willingness to share an arduous journey was a sign of friendship and part of the military oath (Horace imitated these fantastic hyperboles in *Odes* 1.22 and 2.6). The tone changes abruptly with the restrained irony of the litotes *non bona dicta* and the scornful, disgusted sexual language of stanza 5 reinforced by three powerful elisions (the phrase *ilia rumpens* seems not to be obscene, but it is sexually violent). If the poem had ended there, it would have been arresting but it would have fallen short of greatness. However Catullus has another surprise in store for us, in a switch to a more lyrical mode. In epic cut flowers and dead men are sometimes compared; but the flower motif was commoner in wedding songs (e.g. Catullus 62.39ff.; Sappho fragment 105). Catullus is presumably ending his lyric in sapphic metre with an image out of Sappho. Virgil later fused this stanza with a simile in Homer comparing a dead man to a cut poppy for his languorously eroticised picture of the dying Euryalus (*Aeneid* 9.433-7):

> volvitur Euryalus leto, pulchrosque per artus
> it cruor inque umeros cervix conlapsa recumbit;
> purpureus veluti cum flos succisus aratro
> languescit moriens, lassove papavera collo
> demisere caput pluvia cum forte gravantur.

> (Euryalus rolls over in death; over his fair limbs the blood flows and his neck collapses and slumps over his shoulders; as when a purple flower cut from below by the plough languishes as it dies, or poppies droop their heads with tired neck when once weighed down by rain.)

It has been suggested that the passage evokes the defloration of a bride with its attendant bleeding.[46] In Catullus it is the man's love which is pathetically 'deflowered', in ironic reversal[47] (the plough is a figure both for the penis and for civilisation). The flower at the edge of the field picks up the language of limits of the opening stanzas (*extremos, ultimos*).[48] Virgil's lines are vague, opulent, somnolent, smooth, self-indulgent, redolent of a sort of *fin-de-siècle* decadence. By contrast Catullus describes the flower's destruction in a precise and tactile way; we have the cutting *c* and *t* sounds and the unusual elision of *prati* across the line division, mimetic of the cutting. *Tactus* is perfect in sound and sense and in its restraint – a touch is enough. Translations which coarsen the tone ruin the effect (so the Penguin translator, Peter Whigham, has 'slashed' and 'that you, tart, wantonly crushed'). In Catullus all violence of language is drained away in a perfect and perfectly timed diminuendo.'

Charles Martindale, University of Bristol
September 1999

Notes to the Foreword

1. Newman (1990) p. viii.
2. For a particularly hostile review, see D.R. Shackleton-Bailey in *Gnomon* 32 (1960) pp. 775-6 ('ignorance is not this critic's only disqualification'). There were also favourable reviews, e.g. by Michael Putnam, himself to become an influential critic in this tradition, in *Classical Philology* 56 (1961) pp. 204-7. E.J. Kenney (*Classical Review* 11 (1961) pp. 42-3) was characteristically judicious, concluding '*odi et amo*'. Many of Quinn's critics concentrated on the presence of misleading or inaccurate translations, ignoring larger arguments (a characteristic move by the conservative).
3. Mason (1972-5) p. 153.
4. Some scholars argue that the 'correct' form is 'Catullian'; Quinn's preference has, however, proved normative for subsequent usage.
5. Leavis (1962) p. 280.
6. Kermode (1975) in order pp. 163, 170, 164.
7. Brooks (1947) p. 166; cf. p. 1. The further quotations are from pp. 168 and 173.
8. Bahti (1986) p. 213.
9. Leavis (1936) pp. 56, 53. The subsequent quotation is from p. 50.
10. There are passages of what might be called close reading to be found in earlier commentaries, for example the eighteenth-century commentaries on Milton, but necessarily these constitute local insights rather than overall readings.
11. Included in Quinn (1972), pp. 238-42. A particularly early example was Bernard Knox's 'The Serpent and the Flame: The Imagery of the Second Book of the *Aeneid*', first published in 1950 and frequently reprinted. Virgil, Horace, and Catullus were perhaps the poets who responded best to the new approach, Ovid, for example, much less well.
12. More detailed readings will be found in some of Quinn's later publications, in particular his widely used commentary

on Catullus (first published Macmillan 1970, reprinted Bristol Classical Press) and *Catullus: An Interpretation* (1972).

13. Much the same could be claimed of Leavis. Quinn's sub-plot might thus be said to resemble that of *Revaluation*, with Catullus playing a structurally similar role to Leavis' Donne. For literary history as a plot with heroes and villains, see Perkins (1993).

14. For a clear statement of the three main ingredients in the Revolution, see p. 26.

15. Syme inscribes the emergence of the principate as 'revolution'; Quinn's revolution is of course by contrast anti-collective, liberal and individualistic.

16. Conte (1994) p.136; the subsequent quotations are from pp. 144 and 137. For the down-playing of Laelius see Hinds (1998) 77-80; fragment 4 is particularly 'Catullan'. For Quinn's attitude to the issue, see p. 23.

17. For Catullus' reception, see in particular Gaisser (1993); Gillespie (1988); Fitzgerald (1995) pp. 212-35; McPeek (1939); Wiseman (1985) pp. 211-45.

18. The word, always complimentary, is perhaps of somewhat indeterminate meaning, perhaps 'sophisticated' more than 'learned'; see Newman (1990) p. 24.

19. See Gaisser (1993) pp. 272-4. The scholar Muretus did, however, distinguish Catullus' wit from Martial's (Gaisser, p. 201). For Catullus and Martial, see also Newman (1990) ch. 3 and Swann (1994) with the review of William Batstone, *Classical Philology* 93 (1998) pp. 286-9.

20. The identification is based on Apuleius *Apology* 10 (though few follow Apuleius in identifying Virgil's Corydon in *Eclogue* 2 with a slaveboy of Pollio's). Wiseman has raised problems about the traditional identification, proposing instead one of Clodia's sisters, only to produce flawed speculations of his own. The reconstructions are all built on sand, and anyway based on the premiss, which may very well be false, that the poetry is autobiographical. We know almost nothing about the life of Catullus; unfortunately nature abhors a vacuum. Veyne (1988) suggests that Apuleius' identifications might have a different significance for ancient readers than for many moderns, supplying gossip, rather than an opening to the poets' lives and hearts essential for detailed exegesis (p. 174).

21. Poems 1-60 are usually know as the *polymetra*. Jocelyn (1999) protests at the term, and points out that poems 1-60 (to which he plausibly adds 61) fall metrically into three groups: 'Phalaecian' epigrams (hendecasyllables), iambics, and a small number of lyrics. Again one must stress our lack of knowledge. We do not know whether the *Liber Veronensis* is one book or three, nor whether the poet or an editor is responsible for the order. We do not know what was in the collection Martial calls the *Passer Catulli*. This has hardly deterred the critics.

22. For the concept of homosociality see Sedgwick (1985).

23. Significantly, according to Holman Hunt, Catullus was the favourite classical poet of the youthful Dante Gabriel Rossetti, a taste he apparently figures as recherché: 'For Homer he never betrayed great enthusiasm; of the ancients, Catullus was his favourite.... He delighted most in those poems for which the world then had shown but little appreciation (Hunt [1886] p. 738). I owe this reference to Liz Prettejohn.

24. See e.g. Williams (1968) pp. 460-4; Skinner (1971). For the *topoi* of the *renuntiatio amoris*, see Cairns (1972) pp. 80-1.

25. Veyne (1988) pp. 34-5; 174.

26. In ancient terms only a few of Catullus' poems are lyrics. For the application of the idea of lyric to his whole output, see e.g. Johnson (1982) and Miller (1994).

27. 'No other Latin poet appeals so directly and immediately to most modern readers' (Conte [1994] p. 153).

28. Stoppard (1977) pp. 24-5.

29. See Baldwin (1944), vol. 1.

30. See e.g. Fitzgerald (1995) pp. 30-1, where he argues that the idea serves a hidden ideological agenda.

31. See Selden (1992) pp. 464-7; Batstone (1993) p. 150.

32. Newman (1990), who presents a very Bakhtinian Catullus, speaks nicely of a 'carnival use of numbers' (p. 154).

33. Nonetheless Jonson is extraordinarily successful in producing a native English classicism in his version. See Leavis (1936) pp. 18-19: 'Jonson's effort was to feel Catullus, and the others he cultivated, as contemporary with himself; or rather, to achieve an English mode that should express a sense of contemporaneity with them.... This mode...may be described as consciously urbane, mature and civilized. Whatever its relations to any Latin originals, it is indisputably *there*, an achieved actuality.'

34. By contrast Newman (1990) p. 40 sees Catullus as not a love poet but a satirist.

35. Conte (1994) 137; cf. p. 147.

36. Mason (1972-5) p. 173. The subsequent quotation is from p. 178.

37. A start has been made; see e.g. Skinner (1993) and Greene (1998).

38. Batstone *Helios* 20 (1993) p. 83.

39. See Doob (1990).

40. An exception is Ross (1975).

41. Newman (1990) p. 63. See also the review by S.H. Braund in *Journal of Roman Studies* 82 (1992) pp. 247-8.

42. See also the introduction to Parker (1988).

43. Veyne (1988) 112.

44. I owe this formulation to William Batstone. The notion of coherence implied would, of course, be challenged by a Lacanian like Janan, for whom such coherence is always only the object of unattainable desire. Another counter-argument would be that Catullus seems to anticipate so many of the achievements of Augustan poetry, in epic, elegy, and lyric. About Virgil's admiration, in particular, there can be no doubt.

45. See Mayer (1983); Newman (1990) p. 166 sees rather a renunciation of friendship.

46. Fowler (1987).

47. Particularly if we see a sexual subaudition in *penetrabit*.

48. My analysis owes much to a lecture by Denis Feeney.

A number of people have assisted me in formulating this introduction: Will Batstone, David Hopkins, Amanda Kolson, Ellen O'Gorman, Liz Prettejohn, Vanda Zajko. I thank them for discharging *aeternum hoc sanctae foedus amicitiae*.

Bibliography

Adams, J.N., *The Latin Sexual Vocabulary* (Duckworth, 1982).

Bahti, Timothy, 'Ambiguity and Indeterminacy: The Juncture', *Comparative Literature* 38 (1986) pp. 209-23.

Baldwin, T.W., *William Shakspere's Small Latine and Lesse Greeke* (University of Illinois Press, 1944), 2 vols.

Batstone, William, 'Logic, Rhetoric, and Poesis', *Helios* 20 (1993) pp. 143-72 (special *Helios* issue on Catullus).

Bramble, J.C., 'Structure and Ambiguity in Catullus LXIV', *Proceedings of the Cambridge Philological Society* 16 (1970) pp. 22-41.

Brooks, Cleanth, *The Well Wrought Urn: Studies in the Structure of Poetry* (Methuen, 1949).

Cairns, Francis, *Generic Composition in Greek and Roman Poetry* (Edinburgh University Press, 1972).

Clausen, W.V., 'Catullus and Callimachus', *Harvard Studies in Classical Philology* 74 (1970) pp. 85-94.

——'The New Direction in Poetry', in E.J. Kenney and W.V. Clausen (eds), *The Cambridge History of Classical Literature, II, Latin Literature* (Cambridge University Press, 1982) pp. 178-206.

Conte, Gian Biagio, *Latin Literature: A History* (Johns Hopkins University Press, 1994) pp. 136-154.

Doob, Penelope Reed, *The Idea of the Labyrinth from Classical Antiquity through the Middle Ages* (Cornell University Press, 1990).

Feeney, D.C., '"Shall I compare thee...?" Catullus 68B and the Limits of Analogy' in Tony Woodman and Jonathan Powell (eds), *Author and Audience in Latin Literature* (Cambridge University Press, 1992) pp. 33-44.

Fitzgerald,William, *Catullan Provocations: Lyric Poetry and the Drama of Position* (University of California Press, 1995).

Fowler, Don, 'Vergil on Killing Virgins' in Philip Hardie and Michael and Mary Whitby (eds) *Homo Viator: Classical*

Essays for John Bramble (Bristol Classical Press, 1987) pp. 185-198.

Gaisser, Julia Haig, *Catullus and Renaissance Readers* (Oxford Clarendon Press, 1993).

Gillespie, Stuart, *The Poets on the Classics: An Anthology* (Routledge, 1988) pp. 84-9.

Goold, G.P., *Catullus* (Duckworth, 1983), text and translation.

Greene, Ellen, *The Erotics of Domination: Male Desire and the Mistress in Latin Love Poetry* (Johns Hopkins University Press, 1998), chapters 1 and 2.

Hinds, Stephen, *Allusion and Intertext: Dynamics of appropriation in Roman Poetry*, (Cambridge University Press, 1998) pp. 74-83 (on the New Poetry).

Hunt, William Holman, 'The Pre-Raphaelite Brotherhood: A Fight for Art', *The Contemporary Review* 49 (1886) pp. 738-50.

Janan, Micaela, *When The Lamp Is Shattered: Desire and Narrative in Catullus* (Southern Illinois University Press, 1994).

Jenkyns, Richard, 'Catullus and the Idea of a Masterpiece', *Three Classical Poets: Sappho, Catullus, and Juvenal* (Duckworth, 1982) pp. 85-150.

Jocelyn, H.D., 'The Arrangement and the Language of Catullus' So-called *Polymetra* with Special Reference to the Sequence 10-11-12' in J.N. Adams and R.G. Mayer (eds), *Aspects of the Language of Latin Poetry* (Oxford University Press for the British Academy, 1999) pp. 335 -75.

Johnson, W.R., *The Idea of Lyric: Lyric Modes in Ancient and Modern Poetry* (University of California Press, 1982).

Kennedy, Duncan F., *The Arts of Love: five studies in the discourse of Roman love elegy* (Cambridge University Press, 1993).

——'"Cf." Analogies, Relationships and Catullus 68' in Susanna Morton Braund and Roland Mayer (eds), *Amor: Roma. Love and Latin Literature* (*Cambridge Philological Society Supplementary Volume* 22) pp. 30-43.

Kermode, Frank (ed.), *Selected Prose of T.S. Eliot* (Faber and Faber, 1975).

Leavis, F.R., *Revaluation* (Chatto and Windus, 1936).

Leavis, F.R., *The Common Pursuit* (Penguin, 1962, first published 1952).

Lee, Guy, *The Poems of Catullus* (Oxford University Press, 1990), introduction, text and translation.

Lyne, R.O.A.M., 'The Neoteric Poets', *Classical Quarterly* 28 (1978) pp.167-187.

———*The Latin Love Poets: From Catullus to Horace* (Oxford University Press, 1980) pp. 19-61.

Mayer, Roland, 'Catullus' Divorce', *Classical Quarterly* 33 (1983) pp. 297-8.

Mason, H.A., 'Notes on Catullus', *Cambridge Quarterly* 6 (1972-5) pp. 152-178.

McPeek, James A.S., *Catullus in Strange and Distant Britain* (Harvard University Press, 1939).

Miller, Paul Allen, *Lyric Texts and Lyric Consciousness: The Birth of a Genre from Archaic Greece to Augustan Rome* (Routledge, 1994).

Newman, John Kevin, *Roman Catullus and the Modification of the Alexandrian Sensibility* (Wiedmann, 1990).

Parker, W. (ed.), *Priapea: Poems for A Phallic God* (Croom Helm, 1988), introduction and text.

Perkins, D., *Is Literary History Possible?* (Johns Hopkins University Press, 1993).

Quinn, Kenneth (ed.), *Approaches to Catullus* (Heffer, 1972).

———*Catullus: An Interpretation* (Batsford, 1972).

Richlin, Amy, *The Garden of Priapus: Sexuality and Aggression in Roman Humor* (Yale University Press, 1983) pp.144-156.

Ross, David O., *Style and Tradition in Catullus* (Harvard University Press, 1969).

Sedgwick, Eve Kosofsky, *Between Men: English Literature and Male Homosocial Desire* (Columbia University Press, 1985).

Selden, Daniel, '*Ceveat Lector*: Catullus and the Rhetoric of Performance' in D. Selden and R. Hexter (eds), *Innovations of Antiquity* (Routledge, 1992) pp. 461-512.

Skinner, Marilyn, 'Catullus 8: The Comic *Amator* as *Eiron*', *Classical Journal* 66 (1971) pp. 298-305.

Skinner, Marilyn, 'Ego mulier: The Construction of Male Sexuality in Catullus', *Helios* 20 (1993) pp. 107-29.

Stoppard, Tom, *The Invention of Love* (Faber and Faber, 1997).

Swann, Bruce W., *Martial's Catullus: The Reception of an Epigrammatic Rival* (Georg Olms Verlag, 1994).

Vance, Norman, *The Victorians and Ancient Rome* (Blackwell, 1997) pp. 112-132.

Veyne, Paul, *Roman Erotic Elegy: Love, Poetry, and the West* (University of Chicago Press, 1988).

Williams, Gordon, *Tradition and Originality in Roman Poetry* (Oxford University Press, 1968) – use index for particular poems.

Wiseman, Peter, *Catullan Questions* (Leicester University Press, 1969).

——*Cinna the Poet, and Other Essays* (Leicester University Press, 1974).

——*Catullus and His World: A Reappraisal* (Cambridge University Press, 1985).

Preface

THIS book deals mainly with literary criticism. Its object is to assess in general terms the shape of a new movement in poetry that began in Rome around Catullus, and the impact of that movement on the subsequent course of Roman poetry.

The two best books on Catullus in English are A. L. Wheeler's *Catullus and the Traditions of Ancient Poetry* and E. A. Havelock's *The Lyric Genius of Catullus*. The first is now thirty years old, the other twenty, and both have been long out of print. What I have to say has benefited, I hope, from Wheeler's great learning, while my first interest in Catullus (like that of many others) owes much to Havelock, whose book, despite some reckless generalizations, contains much responsive and perceptive criticism. But a good deal has happened in Catullan studies in twenty to thirty years, and a great deal more has taken place in the world of literature in general to change the outlook and standards of the literary critic.

It would have been easy to multiply references. I have tried to keep mine to works that seemed particularly important, or on which I have drawn directly for views that seemed to me novel. The reader who wants some assistance in finding his way more deeply into the literature on Catullus may profitably consult two recent and fairly full bibliographies: that of R. G. C. Levens in *Fifty Years of Classical Scholarship*, edited by M. Platnauer (1955), and J. Granarolo's excellent article, 'Où en sont nos connaissances sur Catulle?' in *L'information littéraire*, 1956, pages 56-65, which is well worth the little trouble it may take to get hold of it. More abundant references, many of them worth following up, will be found in L. Ferrero's *Un' introduzione a Catullo* (1955).

This book began to take shape in my Roman Personal

Poetry Seminar at Melbourne and was written in Cambridge while I was Commonwealth Fellow of St John's College. I am grateful to past members of the Seminar for suggestions and the stimulus they provided, while my particular thanks are due to Professor C. O. Brink, Gonville and Caius College, Cambridge, Professor Thomas Gould, Amherst College, Mass., Dr R. D. Gray, Emmanuel College, Cambridge, and Dr F. R. Leavis, Downing College, Cambridge, for their help and encouragement, and above all to Mr A. G. Lee, St John's College, Cambridge, for detailed and valuable criticism freely given. Finally, but not in the place of least honour, my wife, for her constant support and not inconsiderable collaboration.

The text used for the quotations from Catullus is that of R. A. B. Mynors, Oxford, 1958, by kind permission of Professor Mynors and the Delegates of the Oxford University Press. For convenience, in one corrupt line (Poem 6, 12) I have printed a traditional conjecture.

Robert Graves's poem 'The Cool Web' is reprinted by kind permission of Mr Graves from *Collected Poems 1914-1947*, published by Cassell and Co.

K.Q.

Melbourne
February 1959

For this revised impression a number of minor changes and corrections have been made; the opening pages of Chapter III have been more fully revised, and a paragraph has been added to Chapter I.

A. L. Wheeler's *Catullus and the Traditions of Ancient Poetry* was reprinted in 1964, and a reprint of E. A. Havelock's *The Lyric Genius of Catullus* is in the press.

K.Q.

Dunedin, N.Z.
August 1968

Abbreviations

A.J.Ph.	*American Journal of Philology*
C.Ph.	*Classical Philology*
C.R.	*Classical Review*
F.P.L.	W. Morel, *Fragmenta poetarum latinorum* (1927)
H.St.C.Ph.	*Harvard Studies in Classical Philology*
R.E.L.	*Revue des études latines*
T.A.Ph.A.	*Transactions of the American Philological Association*
Yale Cl.St.	*Yale Classical Studies*

CHAPTER I

The Background

THE relevance of background to a poet's work can be exaggerated. The biographical approach to your author which is traditional in the study of classical literature accords it an importance that many critics today might question. They would not deny the scholar the right to reconstruct by research and speculation all he can of our fragmentary classical heritage. But the different focus they give to their own study of literature might incline them to warn us that preoccupation with the background to a poet's work can make us lose sight of the most important task: to understand, and judge, the work of art itself from the data it itself furnishes and constitutes.[1]

There are many poems of Catullus whose impact upon the modern reader is immediate. Given some experience of poetry in his own language, he need only see how the Latin words fit together, and the sense they make, to have a feeling of contact with first-rate poetry. It is worth while reminding ourselves at the outset of the stature of the poet with whom we have to deal. Consider how the closing lines of Poem 11 climb steeply out of bitter abuse into the purest poetry, the creative impulse transcending the poem's formal objective:

> pauca nuntiate meae puellae
>   non bona dicta.
> cum suis uiuat ualeatque moechis,
> quos simul complexa tenet trecentos,
> nullum amans uere, sed identidem omnium
>   ilia rumpens;
> nec meum respectet, ut ante, amorem,
> qui illius culpa cecidit uelut prati
> ultimi flos, praetereunte postquam
>   tactus aratro est.

No translation can convey the full shock of the final image:

Take a brief harsh message
to her that I loved.
Tell her to live and prosper with her lovers,
and be good riddance—those numberless lechers that share
the embraces of one who loves no man truly, but to all
gives complete satisfaction.
Tell her to forget how I loved her. It meant something
to her once, the love I bore her, that now is like
a flower that hangs snapped, at the meadow's edge,
while the plough passes on.

Or this short passage from Poem 64, also typical, this time of
the way in which the poet's romantic fantasy lingers for a
moment over a detail of his evocation of the heroic past:

quae simul ac rostro uentosum proscidit aequor
tortaque remigio spumis incanuit unda,
emersere freti candenti e gurgite uultus
aequoreae monstrum Nereides admirantes.
illa, atque haud alia, uiderunt luce marinas
mortales oculis nudato corpore Nymphas
nutricum tenus exstantes e gurgite cano.
tum Thetidis Peleus incensus fertur amore.

(Poem 64, 12-19)

Note how this passage is filled with sound, motion and colour:
three verbs (*proscidit, torta, emersere*) suggesting sharp
sound and quick definite motion, plus two other words
(*uentosum, incanuit*) suggesting more continuous, contra-
puntal as it were, combinations of movement and sound—all
in three lines and all in the colours of white foam (*incanuit*)
and the blue expanse of ocean (*aequor*).

The moment the ship's sharp beak cut into the wind-swept
sea,
and her oars twisted the waves into curls of grey-white
foam,
faces rose up from the depths of the radiant ocean:
sea-nymphs come to wonder at the unwonted sight.

2

Not before or since did mortal eyes see their bodies naked,
breasts level with the crest of the glistening spray.
That day, they say, was Peleus fired with love of Thetis.

Proper appreciation of poetry requires, of course, much
more than casual contacts. Yet it is not always obvious how
appreciation will be deepened by the greater grasp that
scholarship offers of things outside the poetry. When we are
confronted with the massive literature on Catullus, the appli-
cation to Catullan studies of the words of an eminent modern
poet and scholar, Mr T. S. Eliot, deserves at very least our
passing consideration:

In my own experience of the appreciation of poetry, I have always
found that the less I knew about the poet and his work, before I began
to read it, the better. . . . . An elaborate preparation of historical and
biographical knowledge has always been to me a barrier.[2]

Having become acquainted, however, in some measure with
a poet, we realize occasionally that we have to deal with a
kind of writing so new that some effort at grasping its overall
nature must be made before we can achieve a proper under-
standing of almost any part of it. Poets vary, moreover, in
the share they take in setting the course that literature will
follow, in their own day and afterwards, and some re-shape
permanently a whole poetic tradition. It is hard to doubt that
Catullus was a poet of this kind. The poetry he wrote is close
in form, style and spirit to much of our own contemporary
poetry and, like our own poetry, it differs sharply in form,
style and spirit from the poetry it largely superseded. It is
this up-to-dateness that makes Catullus popular with us and
causes us to regard him as important.[3] Because of it we ap-
proach the study of his poetry with a sympathy that his inter-
preters in the nineteenth century seem not always to have
possessed. On the other hand, the shape and nature of the
revolution in Roman poetry that Catullus represents tend to
be concealed from us by this very up-to-dateness, in circum-
stances that should instead heighten our interest in their
analysis.

We need not attempt an outline of Roman literary history down to Catullus. That would be a task demanding great scholarship and offering little reward, since for many writers we should have to be content with knowledge so fragmentary that it is little better than ignorance, and almost useless as a basis for critical judgments.[4] What we do need to know is that, at the time when Catullus began to write, there existed elements of poetic tradition distinct from one another and inwardly coherent. To study these elements was the task A. L. Wheeler set himself in his valuable Sather Lectures forty years ago.[5] A shorter, less formalistic review than Wheeler's may still be useful if it helps us to see what Roman poetic tradition had to offer Catullus when he began writing, and how he transformed that tradition. We must, however, from the outset, be on our guard against overstressing the mechanical, deterministic force of tradition, to the neglect of what Mlle A. Guillemin calls 'the human element'. Her words are worth quoting:

La littérature antique se présente à nous comme un système de traditions littéraires dont l'origine se perd dans le lointain des temps. Ces traditions, grandissant par voie de développement, ont fini par peser lourdement sur elle. . . . L'attention des historiens et des philologues, captivée aujourd'hui par l'étude de cette matière, ne cesse de faire des découvertes qui nous ont ouvert mainte perspective. Mais ce gain a pour rançon la mise en oubli des éléments survenant par une tout autre voie: la personnalité de chaque écrivain.[6]

We must also remember, as always in Roman literature, to be circumspect about apportioning credit for innovation: the changed course may be less due to Catullus than now appears and more to other poets whom chance has obliterated. But the change in course is real, nonetheless, and it is worth our while to understand its character.

THE HELLENISTIC BACKGROUND

In the fourth century B.C., the rich and varied tradition of Greek poetry faltered. The fourth is a century rich in philosophers and orators, but not in poets. In so far as it was an age of poetry at all, it followed the tendency of the fifth in concentrating poetic activity on the drama. But Menander and the poets of the New Comedy are small fry, poetically speaking, to set against the giants of the previous century. Outside Athens and outside the drama, there are only such shadowy figures as Timotheus and the girl poet Erinna. One imagines interest in poetry did not die, though we may suspect from Aristotle's *Poetics* it was a kind of interest that prepared the way for the scholarly, historical attitude to poetry of the Hellenistic age and the beginnings of the grammatical tradition It seems to have been chance that silenced the voice of poetry (for the emergence of poetic genius is always a chancy business), rather than lack of interest in poetry, or political decay, which is at least as likely to have the opposite effect. Admittedly, political events such as the creation by Alexander of the splendid new city in Egypt named after him and the efforts of the first Ptolemies to make Alexandria the home of letters and a flowering culture, may well have added impetus to the great fresh wave of poetry with which the third century begins. Half a score of major poets (not dramatists) are familiar to us by their names and known in some measure through their writings. These new Hellenistic poets wrote in an atmosphere of systematic, scholarly study of the old poets: Homer (understandably), Hesiod (whom the Alexandrians seem to have rated higher than we would have expected) and the lyricists. The new poetry, too, was scholarly, written by learned men for learned readers, and this fact could not fail to affect its character. Some of it, the great epic poem of Apollonius for example, leaned heavily on tradition. But much of the new writing was more assertively break-away and devoted to experiment with new forms that were at once more compact and more complex than the old ones.

THE ROMAN BACKGROUND

The Golden Age of this poetic renascence has been set in the half-century 290-240 B.C.[7] The new movement was strongest and richest, therefore, in the years to which tradition assigns

Rome's first fumblings toward literary achievement. Yet it is difficult to discern any obvious connection between the poetry with which Rome began and the poetry that was flourishing in the Hellenistic world other than the link of contemporaneity. Livius Andronicus, the first name in Roman poetry, is representative of the Hellenistic grammarians and scholars and their attitude to literature, but it was the literature of old Greece that he brought to Rome. It is in the old Greek forms, epic and tragedy, that Naevius attempted to create a national literature. There is some evidence that Naevius took the idea of using epic as a vehicle of idealized history from Hellenistic writers, and no reason to suppose there was a water-tight bulkhead isolating the practice of Hellenistic poets from those of old Greece. The two literary ages of Greece, however, are sharply distinct in spirit, and it is the spirit of the old Greek poetry, and the stylistic canons which that spirit implied, that Naevius followed. He differed in this way from Apollonius, for example, the most conservative of the Alexandrians, whose epic is nonetheless the outcome of new attitudes to his subject-matter and to poetry.

With Plautus and Terence came the more recent tradition of Menander and the New Comedy, but the accident that has preserved for us twenty-seven plays by the two writers can mislead us about the course of the main stream of poetic tradition. Rome, at the outset of her literary development, seems clearly to have found epic and tragedy the most congenial forms. It is, after all, understandable that the new, sophisticated, intellectual genres of poetry may have seemed too slender for Ennius, say, to spend much effort on transplanting them to a city only recently quickened to interest in literature, and more easily stirred by sublimity of style and the portrayal of heroic, if shallowly delineated, emotions. From the beginning we find traces of slighter forms (e.g. epigram), but no indication that they found a public prepared to take them seriously as literature. To the 'Father of Roman Poetry', engaged in creating a Roman literature and a national taste, Alexandrianism may have seemed a movement already *passé* (Philetas and Callimachus died probably before Ennius was born, Euphorion probably before he began to write), and one remote geographically from Rome, whose contacts with Greek culture were through the cities of Sicily and Magna Graecia on the one fringe of the Greek world which the empire of Alexander had not reached.

ROMAN POETIC TRADITION BEFORE CATULLUS

Two hundred years roughly separate the beginnings of Roman literature and Hellenistic poetry from the time of Catullus. We can only guess when Catullus began writing. There are two poems that can hardly be later than 60 B.C., neither of which looks like the work of a beginner.[8] Let us take the year 70 B.C., the year Cicero prosecuted Verres, the year Virgil was born, as the nearest round number to the time when Catullus' interest in poetry began to take shape. That is a hundred and seventy years since Livius produced in Rome his (and Rome's) first Latin comedy and tragedy in the year following the close of the first Punic war, and a hundred years since the death of Ennius.

At this point in Roman literary history we can discern three channels that poetic tradition had begun to carve out, by a process of transmutation and original creation, from the mass of inherited material and initial native experiment. The picture is far from clear, and we should remember, if we speak of three channels, that this is a judgment of a literary historian looking back over terrain distant from him and a judgment that might have surprised a contemporary. But sometimes the distant observer sees the lie of the land better than the man on the spot whose attention may be dominated by a single prominent feature.

To an educated Roman in the year 70 B.C. the old epic-tragic tradition must have seemed not only the main stream of poetic tradition, but the only one worth taking seriously. Epic and tragedy were of course distinct as forms, but they shared a common poetic style and a common attitude to their subject-matter, as opposed to the other streams of the tradition. Together they formed the style of serious poetry, and evidence is not lacking that the Romans thought of them as associated in this way. This is the sort of high poetry that Horace has in mind when he talks of the *disiecti membra poetae*[9]—a style that remains unmistakably poetic even if the metre is dislocated. The example of this style quoted by Horace

postquam Discordia taetra
belli ferratos postis portasque refregit

When once foul Strife
had broken open the iron portals of War

(apart from the metre, which Horace specifically leaves out of discussion here) could come equally well from a tragedy or from an epic poem.

Lucretius (writing about 70 B.C.) is a better poet than Ennius had been. Cicero, well launched by this date upon his poetic career, was undoubtedly a worse one in his original compositions, though a highly competent translator. Neither, however, did much to change the style of poetry, or to adapt the poetic language and conventions of a hundred years before. It is worth while glancing back a moment at the fine, dignified rhetoric of Ennius himself, at his impressive language and vivid description of natural scene as well as action, well illustrated in this short extract:

> Incedunt arbusta per alta, securibus caedunt,
> percellunt magnas quercus, exciditur ilex,
> fraxinus frangitur atque abies consternitur alta,
> pinus proceras peruortunt; omne sonabat
> arbustum fremitu siluai frondosai.[10]

They forged on through the lofty forest, hacking their
*   way with axes.*
Great oaks were stricken, the holm oak cut down,
the ash shattered and the tall fir laid low.
They struck down the towering pines. The whole forest
rang with an uproar of timber and foliage.

8

Consider, too, the lofty tone of this fine speech—and the somewhat strip-cartoon heroic character that it builds up for us. Pyrrhus is discussing the return of Roman prisoners:

'Nec mi aurum posco nec mi pretium dederitis:
nec cauponantes bellum sed belligerantes,
ferro non auro, uitam cernamus utrique.
uosne uelit an me regnare era quidue ferat Fors
uirtute experiamur. et hoc simul accipe dictum:
quorum uirtuti belli fortuna pepercit,
eorundem libertati me parcere certum est.
dono, ducite, doque uolentibus cum magnis dis.' [11]

'I ask not for gold, seek not to offer me payment.
Let us each, not peddling war but waging war,
fight to the death, with steel our instrument, not gold.
Are you to reign or I? What is our mistress Fortune's
wish? What has she in store?
Let us valorously put it to the test. And hear this, too,
of me:
These men whose bravery has made them safe from the
fortunes of battle,
their freedom, too, shall be safe, I am resolved.
Take them as my gift. I give them to those who want them,
with the great gods' approval.'

These passages give some notion of the shape and the quality of the epic-tragic tradition. It is a tradition in which the personality of the poet himself is irrelevant. He does not appear in his own person, except for an occasional argument on technical matters of his craft—as happens, too, in the prologues of comedy—and no suggestion of any complexity of attitude towards his subject is permissible.[12] This style was shaped by craftsmen, often foreigners, good at their trade, but not pretending to any insight into the world about them deeper than that needed to manipulate stock types. This was not, of course, the social status of either Lucretius or Cicero, but Lucretius and Cicero, following the main stream of poetic tradition in Rome in their day, accepted the style of these craftsmen-poets.

The epic-tragic tradition is fairly clear-cut. The second stream is more shapeless and incoherent. I shall call it the comic-satiric tradition, though we must be careful not to anticipate too much the future course of Roman literature by talking as though a clearly recognizable comic-satiric tradition existed in and around the year 70 B.C. Little good Roman comedy seems to have been written after Plautus and Terence. In satire, the tradition is even more sporadic. Lucilius seems to have been an isolated figure. Varro of Atax can hardly yet have embarked upon his unsuccessful attempts at writing satire if tradition is right in giving 82 B.C. as the year of his birth, and time seems to have followed Horace in dismissing the nameless others whose failure he records.[13]

The differences of style and attitude which made Roman comedy distinct from tragedy and epic had latent in them the power to contribute to a transformation of Roman poetry. To a Roman living in 70 B.C., it could hardly be apparent what the future held. He was likely to see the past also in a different light. It might well not occur to him, unaware as he was that a new kind of poetry was about to emerge from a regrouping of traditional elements, to connect comedy in any direct way with the tradition of Lucilius and satire.

To Horace, however, writing thirty years later, the connection was clear enough.[14] His first feeling was that the title of poetry should be denied satire altogether:

> neque si qui scribat uti nos
> sermoni propiora, putes hunc esse poetam.
> ingenium cui sit, cui mens diuinior atque os
> magna sonaturum, des nominis huius honorem.[15]

> *And as for the man who like me writes*
> *more as people talk, you can't consider him a poet.*
> *A man needs genius, a mind a little like a god's and lips*
> *to frame high-resounding phrase to be worthy of that name.*

It is not difficult to feel that this definition of poetry is a little ingenuous, and Horace himself quickly realized the poetic possibilities of a style that was less high-flown than epic and tragedy, but more complex in its manner and its attitudes. He gives us later a second, carefully thought-out and carefully phrased statement of the status of satire. Horace's second definition is of particular interest to us because it is at the same time a fair description of the style of much of the poetry of Catullus—though, of course, Horace is thinking only of his own satire in hexameters:

> ergo non satis est risu diducere rictum
> auditoris: et est quaedam tamen hic quoque uirtus:
> est breuitate opus, ut currat sententia, neu se
> impediat uerbis lassas onerantibus auris;
> et sermone opus est modo tristi, saepe iocoso,
> defendente uicem modo rhetoris atque poetae,
> interdum urbani, parcentis uiribus atque
> extenuantis eas consulto.[16]

It is not sufficient then to set your listener laughing,
though there is merit, too, in that. But briefness,
that's essential: it makes your idea flow,
instead of clogging it with words that burden ears already
*   tired.*
Then diction: it must be now austere, now facetious,
playing at times the part of orator or poet,
at times the sophisticated citizen who holds his eloquence
*   in check*
and understates deliberately.

The unity of the comic-satiric tradition, then, lies partly in a kind of general style of writing (more colloquial, more varying in tone), and partly in an overall attitude to the world we live in—its treatment of love, for example, as a comic aberration rather than a tragic mistake. One indication that we are not off the track in looking for more than a linguistic unity between comedy and satire is provided by Horace's regular use of the practice of the Greek comic poets to support his arguments about satire. There is, however, a difference between comedy and satire which is important when considering the relevance of the comic-satiric tradition to Catullus. This is the position in the foreground of interest that Roman republican satire (we find the elements of the tradition re-shaped in Juvenal) accords to the personality of the poet, who is not the anonymous craftsman of epic and the drama, but a person whose status and complex attitudes become part of the subject-matter of his poetry.

The affinity of the comic-satiric tradition to the poetry of Catullus is obvious. It differs, however, from Catullus' poetry in one important respect: its shapelessness and incoherence of form is remote from the exquisite concentration of the new poetry. There is, perhaps, some link to be found in the *cantica* of Plautus, but the real bridge is provided by the third element of the poetic tradition.

For several decades prior to 70 B.C., we find traces of interest in a third kind of poetry, different (like the poetry of the comic-satiric tradition) from the craftsman poetry of epic and tragedy, and occupying different people. The craftsman-poet at Rome needed a *patronus*. The wealthy, politically influential patron of a literary circle became, and remained, a feature of Roman poetry. From such circles the professional poets received, as well as the support of the patron himself, the encouragement and stimulus of contact with an intellectual *élite*, some of whom, maybe, were elegant young men interested in the arts, some *grammatici*—people we should today call 'critics' rather than 'grammarians'.

Not unnaturally, members of these intellectual *élites*, even the *patroni*, began themselves to dabble in poetry. They avoided the professional styles and confined themselves to slighter genres, such as the epigram, that tiny but complete and coherent fragment of a poem which the Alexandrians had brought to a high level of literary excellence. This status as the slightest of all the genres is the position to assign to the small group of often quoted poems preserved for us by Aulus Gellius, the work, or perhaps the play, of Q. Lutatius

12

Catulus, consul of 102 B.C., a leading aristocrat and politician, and of Porcius Licinus and Valerius Aedituus, about whom we shall perhaps not be mistaken if we use the term intellectual *élite*. Four short love epigrams have come down to us ascribed to these three. It may be useful to quote them here in full.[17]

The epigram ascribed to Lutatius Catulus reads:

> Aufugit mi animus; credo, ut solet, ad Theotimum
> deuenit. sic est, perfugium illud habet.
> quid, si non interdixem, ne illunc fugitiuum
> mitteret ad se intro, sed magis eiceret?
> ibimus quaesitum. uerum, ne ipsi teneamur
> formido. quid ago? da, Venus, consilium.

> *My heart has run away from me. Once more, I think, to*
> *Theotimus*
> *it has gone. Yes, it has taken refuge there.*
> *What if I had not forbidden him to admit*
> *the refugee, but to throw him out instead?*
> *Let us go and seek him out. Though I am afraid*
> *I may be detained myself. What shall I do? Advise me,*
> *Venus, do.*

We have two epigrams by Valerius Aedituus: the first is an attempt to describe the physical sensation of being violently in love (compare Catullus, Poem 51; Horace, *Odes* I. 13):

> Dicere cum conor curam tibi, Pamphila, cordis,
> quid mi abs te quaeram, uerba labris abeunt,
> per pectus manat subito subido mihi sudor:
> sic tacitus, subidus, dum pudeo, pereo.

The text of the second couplet is far from certain.

> *When, Pamphila, I try to tell you of the pain in my heart,*
> *the words fail on my lips, to say what I want of you.*
> *My breast is damp with sudden sweat. I am confused.*
> *Silent, confused, I am ashamed and tortured.*

The second epigram of Aedituus elaborates a conceit:

Quid faculam praefers, Phileros, quae nil opus nobis?
 ibimus sic, lucet pectore flamma satis.
istam nam potis est uis saeua extinguere uenti
 aut imber caelo candidus praecipitans;
at contra hunc ignem Veneris nisi si Venus ipsa
 nulla est quae possit uis alia opprimere.

Why bear a torch before us, Phileros, we have no need of it?
We will go as we are. My breast provides sufficient flame.
Your flame the raging wind is able to extinguish,
or the bright rain that teams from heaven.
But this fire that Venus lit, no power on earth,
unless herself, can quench it.

The epigram of Porcius Licinus toys with a similar conceit:

Custodes ouium tenerae propaginis, agnum,
 quaeritis ignem? ite huc; quaeritis? ignis homost.
si digito attigero, incendam siluam simul omnem.
 omne pecus flammast, omnia quae uideo.

You who guard the tender race of sheep and lambs,
you want a fire? Come to me. Are you surprised? The flame
is I.
A touch from my finger and the whole forest blazes,
your whole flock flames, all my eye falls on.

In addition we have from various sources three short poems
dealing with literary criticism and personalities. Firstly, an
epigram by Catulus on Roscius:

Constiteram exorientem Auroram forte salutans,
 cum subito a laeua Roscius exoritur.
pace mihi liceat, caelestes, dicere uestra:
 mortalis uisus pulchrior esse deo.

I stopped by chance to greet the rising dawn.
Suddenly on my left Roscius rose.
Dwellers in the sky, may I say it?
The mortal seemed fairer to me than the divinity.

Then two pieces ascribed to Licinus, neither of them in the elegiac metre used in the little poems so far considered. One is a two-line epigram:

> Poenico bello secundo Musa pinnato gradu
> intulit se bellicosam in Romuli gentem feram.

In the second Punic war the Muse with winged course invaded the savage, war-like Roman race.

The other is a fragment, apparently, of a longer work. Its subject is the comedian Terence. In it Licinus confuses (as critics still do occasionally) literary criticism with unsavoury gossip. The text is uncertain and the piece, since it has no poetic merit, need not delay us here. Our concern is with the four love epigrams. These elegant, but hard, trifles dealing with love, but dealing with it with a cold, unreal ingenuity that emphasizes their Greek inspiration, seem remote from Catullus and the subsequent course of Roman personal poetry, but they represent the first steps in a new direction.

The fragments of Laevius are of a rather different order. There is much more to them—some thirty fragments varying from a single line to half a dozen lines, torn for the most part from a context, usually a dramatic one, and not always making much sense now that the context has been lost. There is great metrical variety, so that, from the point of view of metre, they foreshadow the first section of Catullus' book, whereas the elegiac epigrams of Lutatius Catulus and the others foreshadow the last section. It will be sufficient to quote one piece which appears complete in itself, and to give in the notes to this chapter the Latin text of the remaining fragments.[18] The poem seems to be addressed to a garland of flowers:

> te Andromacha per ludum manu
> lasciuola ac tenellula
> capiti meo, trepidans libens,
> insolita plexit munera.

With her hands Andromacha, for sport,
those tender, playful little hands,
eager and excited, for my head
wove you, extraordinary gift.

Constantly, in this last group of writers, we find hints of something it is not perhaps an exaggeration to consider as an important third element in the Roman poetic tradition which the genius of Catullus absorbed and re-shaped. The whole of what we have of this third element amounts to very little, compared with the more substantial fragments and the quite large group of complete works offered us by the other two streams of the tradition. There never was very much, perhaps, to the third element until Catullus. These little poems represent nonetheless the first steps towards creating a Roman genre out of the Greek epigram. Even when they are largely imitative, these poets are facing up to problems of expression, of finding how to say new things in Latin. It was left to Catullus to utilize their experiments in technique in writing real poetry.

The reader need hardly be warned against taking this brief review of general trends as though it were intended to be systematic and exhaustive. Its purpose is only to give a rough indication of the state of poetry when Catullus began to write. Even doing that has taken us some time, and it would perhaps be useful to consider, in the very briefest space, what Catullus took from each of these three streams of tradition in order to embody it in a fresh synthesis.

The most important contribution of the epic-tragic tradition is the status it had won for Roman poetry as serious literature. The mere practice of poetry, of course, over a couple of centuries had done much to prepare the Latin language for very different poetic uses. Catullus at least once imitates Ennius directly and at some length.[19] But much more important than the occasional direct imitation is the fact that the epic and tragic poets had worked out in general terms the way to describe a scene, the way to study emotion with dignity and pathos, and the words to use.[20]

16

From the comic-satiric tradition the Catullan movement was able to transplant into serious poetry a fresh directness and simplicity of language. The new poets drew upon this tradition further for their frank studies of individuals and their shortcomings. This stream provided not only realism of this kind, but also idealizations of love as an important activity, and of youth and friendship in opposition to old men and old men's notions of what constitutes the serious business of life. Finally, comedy, or Plautus at any rate, provided some sort of precedent for metrical experiment and variety.

From the third stream of tradition, which we have made up from epigram and the polymetric fragments, came a sense of exquisite form and the technique of making a ruthless selection of detail in order to suggest a story by a few touches, instead of telling it at length. From the epigrams in particular came a new status for poetry as a painstaking exercise in self-expression, divorced from the task of instructing, or even entertaining, the community as a whole.

This is not the whole story and it would be easy to add details under each head. There is obviously also a measure of interaction between the three streams. But with these reservations we may say these are the elements which represent the continuity of poetic tradition in Catullus. Against them we have to set the individual genius of the poet himself, and the impact on poetry of changing social factors, particularly the new status in society of the poet which Catullus and those around him demanded. We must not expect to explain Catullus by tabulating traditional and social factors, but, having set these out, we can see better what happened when Catullus appeared in Roman poetry.

Another omission—it may appear almost perverse—is to have said nothing of the classical and Alexandrian Greek writers on whom Catullus drew. My reason is that in this section I have tried to confine myself strictly to the question: What had the Roman literary tradition to offer Catullus, in terms of styles of poetry, and by way of technical accomplishment, when he began writing? That is what we most need to know, in order to assess the nature of the Catullan revolution. The Roman tradition was based, and frequently refounded on the Greek, though it was never as purely derivative as was once supposed, and Catullus himself drew widely on his extensive knowledge of Greek poetry.[21] Consequently we shall blur the shape of the Catullan revolution if we do not keep three factors separate from one another in our minds. They are: the contribution of the Roman tradition; the contribution made by the poets of the Catullan revolution from their own resources of genius, environment and outlook; and, thirdly, the extent to which these two factors were enriched by borrowings from a closely connected, more highly developed, but nonetheless alien poetic tradition.[22]

Scholars are less disposed today than at the turn of the century to write off a Latin poem as 'obviously taken from the Greek'—even if they could not produce the original. Few now take seriously Wilamowitz' theory (argued in detail in 1879, re-stated in modified form in 1924) that Catullus' *Attis* (Poem 63) is a translation, or at any rate a close imitation, of an Alexandrian original, conjured into existence and fathered upon Callimachus on the strength of a two-line fragment of uncertain authorship in the same metre but making no mention of Attis. W. Y. Sellar seems to us to talk better sense when he wrote (a century ago) 'there is nothing at all like the spirit of this poem in extant Greek literature' (*Roman Poets of the Republic*, 1863, p. 369). A poem of Catullus may recall Greek originals and remain a Roman poem: Poem 70, for example, sets out from an epigram of Callimachus (25.1-4 Pf) and ends with an echo of Sophocles (fragment 741 N); yet what could be more characteristically Catullus, or more completely a Roman poem?

CHAPTER II

The Tradition Re-shaped

THE previous chapter had two objects: to assess roughly what in the poetry of Catullus we may attribute to the shaping force of Roman poetic tradition, and to show the complexity of that tradition and the interconnection between its elements.

It will not have escaped the reader familiar with critical writing on Catullus that a different emphasis is given to the factor of tradition by what may be called the common view. One reason indeed for a critical reassessment of Catullus is that Catullus, more than the general run of ancient writers, has been made the subject of widely-entertained, but hardly tenable generalizations.

The common view may be summarized briefly. Firstly, Catullus' 'models' (as classical criticism likes to call the writers who shape the poetry even of a genuinely creative poet) are Greek, and in particular Alexandrian, not Roman. Secondly, only the epigrams of the 'circle' of Lutatius Catulus and the fragments of Laevius provide any link between Catullus and antecedent Roman poetry.[1] The purpose of this chapter is to examine these two generalizations.

To take the first: as stated, there is a *naïveté* in the sound of it that I may be suspected of introducing to facilitate attack. It is not difficult, however, to quote leading Catullan critics who put their case as simply as this. A. L. Wheeler said for example:

Catullus and many of his contemporaries neglected—Cicero's word is 'despised'—that part of their heritage which was Roman. . . . When he sought aid from the past, he turned directly to the Greeks.[2]

Much is often made of the passage from the *Tusculan Disputations* (III. 45) to which Wheeler alludes. The passage deserves a fresh scrutiny, for it is often assumed to prove more than it does. After quoting a couple of passages in epic-tragic style from the *Andromacha* of Ennius, Cicero exclaims:

O poetam egregium! quamquam ab his cantoribus Euphorionis contemnitur.
What a remarkable poet! These singers of the praises of Euphorion grossly underrate him.

The sense of *cantores* as a critical term is to some extent fixed by a passage from Horace written a few years later:

quos neque pulcher
Hermogenes umquam legit, neque simius iste
nil praeter Caluum et doctus cantare Catullum.[3]

But our friend Hermogenes has never read these people [the writers of Old Comedy], *any more than that ape who never learnt anything except how to sing the praises of Calvus and Catullus.*

Horace obviously agreed with Cicero in his opinion of the successors of Catullus, though elsewhere he by no means endorses Cicero's high opinion of the old Roman writers.

Ennius' lines are charged with emotion. Cicero's critical comment is also expressed in emotional form, though Wheeler's 'despised' is perhaps an over-translation. After all, if we translate instead 'grossly underrated', it would not greatly surprise us if Cicero had said of Horace (supposing he had lived long enough to be familiar with Horace's poetry) what he says here of the *cantores Euphorionis*.[4] Cicero was, or had become by the time of the *Tusculans* (which he wrote in the last years of his life), well known for his support of old Roman literature, whereas Horace twenty-five years later underrated it with such emphasis that literary historians are still occasionally trapped into accepting his remarks uncritically.[5]

The usual interpretation, moreover, possibly misses part of the point of Cicero's remark. It has been suggested[6] that what distinguished Euphorion among the Alexandrians was

20

the extreme form of verbal poetry, the excessively conscious verbal artistry which he practised, and that the nearest Roman equivalent to his style is to be found in the heavily descriptive passages of Catullus, Poem 64. And, indeed, the last passage from Ennius quoted by Cicero

> O pater, o patria, o Priami domus,
> saeptum altisono cardine templum!
> uidi ego te, astante ope barbarica,
> tectis caelatis laqueatis
> auro ebore instructam regifice.

> *My father! land of my fathers! palace of Priam!*
> *temple sealed with doors that swung with high-pitched*
> *   hinges' creak!*
> *I saw the invading barbarian host*
> *(above them the chiselled, fretted ceilings)*
> *within that royal fabric of ivory and gold.*

approaches the mannered descriptive style of Catullus, Poem 64. The metre, of course, is different, and the archaic dignity is natural to the poet, and not (as in Catullus, Poem 64) a device of art to evoke the atmosphere of the heroic past. The lamentations of Andromacha might well recall those of Ariadne. This does not mean Catullus was an imitator of Ennius, but that he utilized to the full the resources of tradition, sometimes even by distorting the spirit of the poetry he drew upon. This seems at any rate the way Catullus has handled Ennius in the one passage where we can point to sustained imitation.[7] So that Cicero may, in effect, have at the back of his mind some such thought as this: 'The *poetae novi* turn their noses up at Ennius, but he can do that sort of thing as well as they can.' The phrase *cantores Euphorionis* is not meant, of course, to be other than uncomplimentary[8], but though Cicero obviously disapproved of the *poetae novi* (more specifically the *successors* of Catullus: *his* implies living contemporaries, whereas Catullus had been dead for something like a decade), his instinct for literature made him sense all the same a continuity of tradition that the *cantores Euphorionis* were likely enough reluctant to acknowledge.

In E. A. Havelock's *The Lyric Genius of Catullus*, published in 1939, the accuracy of the common view is repeatedly taken for granted. It is particularly surprising that a critic as sympathetic and as enthusiastic as Havelock shows himself to be should not have stressed more Catullus' originality as a poet and the magnitude of his achievement in re-shaping a complex tradition. To hold that Catullus is an Alexandrian by cultural upbringing, or at any rate uniformly Greek in inspiration (Havelock allows a wider range of Greek influence than some critics), overlooks two vital factors. Firstly, Catullus' formal indebtedness to Roman tradition and the role played in shaping his poetry by the poet's own temperament, which is so un-Greek. Secondly, his status in society, which is Roman and arises from Roman traditions such as the literary circle and the position in it of the writer of *satura*.

The common view neglects, too, the part played by the contemporary Roman milieu in which Catullus lived. The significance of this brings us to the second aspect of the common view. Where Wheeler does admit Roman tradition, it is that of the amatory epigrammatists who followed the Alexandrian tradition closely: Lutatius Catulus, Valerius Aedituus and Porcius Licinus. Their highly interesting little poems, as the previous chapter showed, are undoubtedly one of the streams of the tradition. They provide the first specimens we have of the integrated small-scale poem in Latin. Their subject is the poet himself, though this personal reference is still devoid of worth-while personal emotion. It springs rather from a convention of the epigram, where the briefest possible factual basis is arrived at, in order to permit maximum concision. It is obviously more economical of space to use a speaker in the first person. To name and introduce a speaker (unless he is needed as a *personality*) is wasteful of space. But the technique is a far cry from charging speech in the first person with a highly personal, or deeply felt, attitude to what is said.

22

We must not allow obvious small affinities to cause us to exaggerate the role played by these epigrams in bringing into being the very genuine poetry of Catullus. Poems written in the same metrical and stylistic form can be nonetheless so widely separated in their status and quality as poetry, or in the measure of seriousness accorded them by the poet (both in the degree of his artistic involvement and the degree of his emotional involvement in his subject), that it is almost idle to talk of connections between them. It is an excessively formalistic approach that led Wheeler, it seems to me, to underestimate the gulf separating the early trifles from the front-rank poetry of the school of Catullus. If we regard the *poetae novi* as the culminating point of an evolution that began perhaps half a century earlier, we underrate the revolution which broke out round Catullus. There is always a measure of continuity in literature, even in literary revolutions. But revolutions do occur, they can break out suddenly, and their significance can be missed by looking too closely at the formal features that survive and by neglecting the new spiritual atmosphere that pervades them.

The short witticism in verse and the well-turned trifle are the natural by-products of poetry wherever it is practised. Nor is it uncommon for the educated public figure or man of leisure, whose interests in poetry are as reader or patron but not as writer, to vie (on this low level) with the professional poets who are his associates or his protégés. A century and a half after the death of Catullus we find the younger Pliny toying with poetry in this way and justifying himself by citing[9] a long list of prominent figures in Roman history (including Q. Lutatius Catulus) who did the same. Both here: 'utque omnia innoxiae remissionis genera breuiter amplectar',[10] and in another place, 'His [i.e. hendecasyllabis nostris] iocamur, ludimus, amamus, dolemus, querimur, irascimur',[11] Pliny is at pains to make it clear that he is not a professional poet.

In an age where sophistication outruns talent (as it often did in Hellenistic times), such by-products tend to choke out

23

the real article. The revolution that the *poetae novi* represent is not explained by pointing to their interest in epigram and *vers de société*, or to those poems of Catullus which, if there were not others, might make him indeed look like a successor of Catulus and the epigrammatists. What has to be explained is that the verse that the *poetae novi* still called *nugae* (accepting the depreciatory title as a challenge) became for them, not the marginal by-products of genius in moments of relaxation, but the vehicle of a new kind of poetry. They clearly took it very seriously and, largely because of this seriousness, they brought it to an unprecedented and unforeseeable level of artistic quality. There is a fundamental shift in emphasis which progressively changed the whole nature of their poetry; excessive preoccupation with continuity can obscure not only the reason for this change, but its artistic consequences as well.

The gap between Laevius and Catullus is not appreciably narrower—as far as we can tell. The technical contribution is clear from the fragments, and it is of a kind rather different from the contribution of the epigrammatists, lying more in language than in theme, and in a new lightness of note. But we must remember we have no complete poem of Laevius, however short, and no fragment clearly pointing to a greater measure of personal involvement than existed, probably, in the verses referred to by Catullus in Poem 50. It should be obvious that those poems of Catullus which we rank seriously as poetry were the outcome of different circumstances and attitudes from those hours he spent with Licinius Calvus, however stimulating he found them. At the risk, necessarily, of being unfair to Laevius, we must say the fragments give no indication of the revolution in the whole attitude to poetry that made the movement of the *poetae novi* what it was.

The phenomenon is perhaps primarily a social one. From this point onwards in Roman literature, until at any rate the end of the Augustan age, poets ceased to be the craftsmen-protégés of sophisticated noblemen. We have now to deal instead with people either (like Catullus) possessing a high degree of independence,[12] or (like Horace and Propertius a generation later) demanding this independence from their patron. The repeated polite refusals of the Augustan personal poets to write epic represent clearly their determination to retain the new independence the Catullan movement had won for poetry, and their determination that poetry should not again be at the beck and call of statesmen and generals.

Being independent, poets could now expect the community to be interested in them and their doings as people. If the community was not interested, they were in a position not to care and to go on writing all the same. They were not any more anonymous mouthpieces of the community, but individuals determined to set, not simply to accept, the standards of the community; or, if they could not, to defy the community. The great artist is prepared to be the impersonal tool of his community in moments of national greatness when he can sincerely share its ideals. Rome must have felt herself to be passing through such moments often in the third and second centuries, and again perhaps for the first decade after the battle of Actium. In times, however, of national disintegration or disillusionment poets may either assail their community with advice or abuse (as English poets of the twenties and thirties did, and as Horace tried occasionally to do), or withdraw from the community (like many of our contemporary poets). A comparable social disintegration separates the contemporaries of Catulus from those of Catullus. It produced Lucretius, who tried to advise his contemporaries, and the *poetae novi*, who occasionally abused, but mostly disregarded, the man in the street:

> istos, qui in platea modo huc modo illuc
> in re praetereunt sua occupati.
> (Poem 15, 7-8)
> *those who in the streets move up and down,*
> *their own affairs absorbing them.*

When this happens, it often happens also that the large poem, which impresses the community by its extent and its sublimity, is displaced by the short poem where concise craftsmanship, intellectual distinction and ability to handle form are more apparent, though apparent primarily to an inner circle.

These are the three ingredients involved in the re-shaping of tradition that produced the Catullan revolution. Firstly, the poet becomes an independent personality who forces his personality into his poetry. Secondly, the poet abandons the service of the community for a more esoteric, more purely poetic kind of poetry. Thirdly, the unit becomes the short poem, intensely personal and structurally sophisticated. The poems of Catullus are usually the length, roughly, of modern lyrics. A few are a good deal longer (the longest has four hundred and eight lines), and it seems other *poetae novi* wrote long poems, too, e.g. the *Zmyrna* of Cinna referred to in Poem 95, or Caecilius' poem referred to in Poem 35. These longer poems are, however, quite different from epic: they are capable still of being read, or heard, and their complex structure appreciated (after a good deal of preliminary study perhaps) at a single sitting.

Of these three ingredients, the second and third reflect in some measure trends in Hellenistic poetry and there are obvious similarities between the Hellenistic poets and the *poetae novi*. The first is not present in Hellenistic poetry to anything like the same extent, for the social disintegration of the Hellenistic age produced a more complete despair of society and a more passive escapism than the social upheavals of the last century of the Republic, which aroused stronger, less decadent emotions, emotions more useful to poetry. Moreover, the Hellenistic age failed to secure the link between poetry and the ruling classes of society that brought about the emergence, from Catullus on to Horace, of the poet as an independent worth-while personality. In this sense the Alexandrian age of Roman poetry did not come until Nero.

CHAPTER III

Levels of Intent

ORMATIVE influences are not everything. We must be on our guard against taking it for granted that the poetry these influences shaped was of a single kind. This is, in fact, often assumed. One reason for the assumption is that a dozen or so short poems are so familiar we tend to have only them in mind when we think in general terms of the poetry of Catullus. Assuming then that Catullus is typical of the whole movement, we talk as though the new poetry possessed a single style, sprang from a single kind of aspiration, and was even uniform in quality into the bargain.

Yet if we read the Catullan collection right through, even casually, it is plain at once that it consists of very different kinds of poetry. Obviously the long poems in the centre of the collection, especially Poems 63 and 64, are very unlike the rest. But even the short poems can hardly fail to strike us as representing a number of different types of writing.

No worth-while poet, of course, goes on doing exactly the same thing in poem after poem, and not even the best poets write every time with equal success. But with Catullus the differences, even among the short poems, are sharp enough for the sensitive reader to feel that something is involved which he has to think about right from the beginning of his appraisal of the poet's work. If, in reading these short poems, we received instead the impression that the degree of unlikeness we noted was only of the order that we find, for example, between different odes of Horace or different elegies of Propertius, we could afford to postpone our consideration of these differences until we had come more closely to grips with our author. We might in that case turn our attention first to the question whether the long poems are as distinct from the short poems as, say, the satires of Horace are from the odes,

27

or whether the differences are more like the differences between the aetiological poems of the fourth book of Propertius and his earlier elegies.

To return to Catullus. We have, in effect, to make up our minds on two counts. Let us formulate the issues in precise terms. Firstly, do the short poems represent a variety of types of writing that is unusual in the work of a single poet? If we feel they do, we should try to decide how before turning to the second question, which is: are the long poems (apart from being longer) fundamentally different from all the short ones?

One reason why these are important points at which to begin considering the poetry of Catullus is that on each of these questions there exists once again, particularly among critics writing in English, what may be called a common view. It is one the sensitive reader today (as opposed to the reader of a couple of decades ago) may find hard to accept. Briefly, the common view involves answering our first question with 'no' and the second with 'yes'. I think the common view is wrong on both counts.

On the first, the common view owes its currency in large measure to E. A. Havelock's brilliant statement of it thirty years ago:

The total of a hundred and nine poems and fragments deserves to be regarded as a single body of work, displaying certain common characteristics of style and substance, the work in fact of a lyric poet.[1]

This is the central thesis of Havelock's book, repeated a number of times in differing terms in the course of his argument.[2] Yet our reaction, if we read the hundred and nine short poems ourselves, is surely that this is simply not so. We might almost suspect Havelock of basing his thesis really, not on the hundred and nine, but on the twenty-six poems he selects to discuss and translate. But I think we interpret Havelock more fairly if we say that he uses the term 'lyric' less as a judgment of style (despite his words just quoted) or of the formal qualities of the poems, than as a description of the impulse that, in his view, produced them. An impulse, we may say, fired by genius, to translate emotion into spontaneous song. In fact, Havelock's view of the unity of the poems rests on the assumption that they are the *work* of a lyric poet. It is an intuition about the poet rather than a judgment of his poetry, an intuition, incidentally, whose rigid application occasionally leads Havelock into dogmatic generalizations, such as the following:

his genius [is] lyrical, in the sense that he could not write anything significant which was not essentially a quick mood expressed within narrow limits.[3]

Havelock's thesis, therefore, is that the short poems are great poetry in so far as they lend themselves to the expression of the poet's essential genius. In other words, he has given us, if my stricter statement of it represents his thesis fairly, something that is much less positive criticism of the poems as we have them than is usually supposed, though it is only fair to add at once that the book contains much sensitive and discerning criticism of the poetry of Catullus, some of it hard to reconcile with the book's central thesis.

If Havelock had developed his thesis, he might have considered such interesting questions as the degree to which, even in the short poems, the inherited formal characteristics of the various genres which Catullus adopted impeded his lyric genius; or the degree to which Catullus, by not being properly conscious of the essential nature of his own genius, frustrated it by attempting styles of writing (for example, the imageless, intellectual style of the elegiac poems) to which it was unsuited. A combination of this kind of approach with that of A. L. Wheeler might have made very stimulating reading. As it is, I am not sure that *The Lyric Genius of Catullus* takes us very far towards understanding the poems that we actually have.

The long poems, on the other hand (to pass to our second question), seem, by their whole scale and nature, condemned *a priori* if one believes that Catullus' genius was exclusively lyrical. The common opinion, at all events, is that they are failures.

The view that there are *two* Catulluses, a simple lyric poet and an artificial bookish poet, has long been a familiar one. The standard commentator on Catullus, Wilhelm Kroll, writing in 1922, expresses the dichotomy with a vigorous succinctness worth attempting to recapture in English:

In the first place, there are two aspects of Catullus: there is the Alexandrian weighed down by the burden of tradition, and there is the spontaneous, primitive child of nature.[4]

It has been equally usual to assume that Alexandrianism means bad writing. Consider the following assessment, which is to be found in a standard work of reference:

Alexandrian influence was strong in his circle. The epithet *doctus* applied to him later . . . practically means Alexandrian. . . . He avoids, however, the worst Alexandrian faults: obscurity, over-cleverness, excess of erudition, and allusiveness.[5]

Clearly the implication is that obscurity, cleverness, erudition and allusiveness are undesirable in poetry and that Catullus' poetry is saved only by not indulging in these faults too much.

Havelock resists the notion of two Catulluses: he finds it 'risky to assume that a poet's muse can thus be partitioned' (p. 76); for him there is only one Catullus—the lyric poet. The long poems get pretty short shrift: the writing is 'significant and important only in so far as it is lyrical' (p. 78); there is something to be said for 61 and 63, precious little for 64, nothing at all for 65 and 68. As far as the Catullan *oeuvre* is concerned, therefore, there are really two Catulluses after all—one good and one bad.

It is not difficult to discern in the common view vestiges of the cant of romantic criticism and the loose assumption that the true lyric poet, like Shelley's skylark, pours his full heart in profuse strains of unpremeditated art. What is *doctus*, it is asserted, cannot be lyric. So that this epithet, which antiquity repeatedly applied to Catullus, must be confined to sections of his work that are not lyrical, and bad.

We do not have to align ourselves with those today who would welcome wholeheartedly obscurity, cleverness, erudition and allusiveness among the constituents of a good poem (instead of listing them among the graver faults) in order to feel that the presence of these elements in the long poems does not necessarily spoil the poetry. A more fundamental readjustment of the common view is called for, however, if the same learned elements can be shown to exist, in significant proportion, in the short poems. A certain amount of recent work in this direction[6] points fairly unequivocally to the view that, in most of his book, Havelock underrates the complexity of the process of making a short Catullan poem.

It is only fair to remember Havelock's book is now thirty years old and, to judge from the poetic style of his translations, based on a taste moulded at least a decade earlier. Moreover, Havelock is too sensitive a critic to adhere rigidly to some of his own more extreme statements. For example, on page 183 he writes that 'Catullus is all emotion'. Elsewhere he allows Catullus an exquisite sense of form, but here in his enthusiasm for emotion, he derides this formal precision as the 'tight thin glove of contemporary fashion'. A chapter on Catullus' learning, *'Doctus Catullus*—the Master of Form' is very sound, perhaps the best in the book. But much of it is highly inconsistent with the judgment of the long poems which the central argument of the book requires.

One should obviously not attempt to deny that the poems vary considerably in the degree to which they wear their *doctrina* on the surface, or to argue that the common view is wholly unfounded. Poem 50, for example, which must have been written in an hour or so, clearly differs enormously in the process of its composition from Poem 64. The objections to the common view are these. Firstly, that the slogan of the two Catulluses, adopted, really, after all by Havelock (as his condemnation of the long poems shows), rests on too gross a simplification. Whatever truth there is behind the dichotomy is insufficient to justify its use—as it has been used—as a major tool of Catullan criticism. Indeed the term Alexandrian, once we become reluctant to accept it as simply pejorative, loses a good deal of its critical significance. Secondly, we should object that, when Havelock calls the short poems the work of a lyric poet, he is offering us what may well be a perceptive intuition of the poet's temperament, but one that is often likely to provide a precarious and inadequate criterion for judging what Catullus actually wrote. It is as if we said of a painter who spends much of his time on abstracts and landscapes that his genius is essentially for portraiture. However discerning the statement might be, obviously it is only a beginning, and, in dealing with particular pictures, may actually launch the critic on the wrong track.

Because we are not prepared to chop the poetry of Catullus into two chunks, however, one good and one bad, we do not have to suppress our first reaction to Catullus' little book: that it is made up of kinds, several kinds, of poetry which seem somehow essentially different. It is difficult not to feel that we have to deal with something more than the usual differences in form or in subject-matter, or between early and late work, or simply between varying degrees of success and failure.

A useful way of dealing with our reaction to the poems is to think in terms of what may be called differing *levels of intent,* differing degrees of devotion to the task of making poetry, varying, in the case of Catullus, from the most casual versifying to the most complete surrender to inspiration. This notion of the level of poetic intent is quite unusually important in studying Catullus. The internal evidence of the poems alone seems to point clearly to different kinds of writing, involving different degrees of poetic endeavour, envisaging different kinds of audience, to an extent that is uncommon in the permanently surviving work of any poet. We feel certainly something very different from the uniform intended-for-serious-publication note that dominates subsequent Roman personal poetry.

Let us consider some examples illustrating this range of level, before we try to find reasons for it. On the lowest level, that of the most restricted and of the least ambitious intent (judging intent strictly on internal evidence, not on supposed

facts about the poet's life), are the short poems of savage
invective. Take Poem 59:

> Bononiensis Rufa Rufulum fellat,
> uxor Meneni, saepe quam in sepulcretis
> uidistis ipso rapere de rogo cenam,
> cum deuolutum ex igne prosequens panem
> ab semiraso tunderetur ustore.

The first line has a kind of lapidary, or rather graffital,
finality. Indeed similar graffiti have been found at Pompeii,
e.g.:

> Saluia felat Antiocu/luscu.[7]

Martial tells us that prostitutes used to frequent graveyards.
In the last line *tunderetur* is perhaps therefore ambiguous.
(Cf. Mart. I. 34. 8; III. 93. 15.)

> *Rufa from Bologna stoops to oblige her Rufulus.*
> *Menenius' wife I mean. Often in the graveyards*
> *you've seen her grabbing up for dinner a lump of bread*
> *that's tumbled from the pyre's flames. As she chases it*
> *the half-shaved slave in charge lays into her.*

We have not to guess the precise intent of poems like this
one to see the level of poetry they represent. Sometimes it
will be the private working-off of fury, sometimes this shared
with a few friends, sometimes some more public form of
ridicule, sometimes, perhaps, the 'stratégie amoureuse où tous
les coups semblaient permis pour triompher d'un dangereux
concurrent' that a French scholar has seen as the unifying
intent of the Gellius epigrams.[8]

If we remember we are judging poetry, not writing bio-
graphy, we can concentrate on what is for us the most im-
portant inference: that in these poems Catullus' poetic intent
was at its lowest level. This is not a moral judgment, of
course, but a literary one. The poems of which the one I
have quoted is a sample have qualities that can make us glad
they have been preserved: intensity, an instinct for the telling
use of language, and a lively imaginativeness in their ob-

scenity. But to suppose Catullus intended them to be taken as poetry, on anything approaching the level of the best known Lesbia poems, is surely absurd.

Contrast with these vituperative trifles (one in five, perhaps, of the total) a group of longer poems written in seriously poetic language, possessing qualities of structure and imagination that clearly put them on a different level of poetic intent. The well known Poem 31 is typical:

> Paene insularum, Sirmio, insularumque
> ocelle, quascumque in liquentibus stagnis
> marique uasto fert uterque Neptunus,
> quam te libenter quamque laetus inuiso,
> uix mi ipse credens Thuniam atque Bithunos
> liquisse campos et uidere te in tuto.
> o quid solutis est beatius curis,
> cum mens onus reponit, ac peregrino
> labore fessi uenimus larem ad nostrum,
> desideratoque acquiescimus lecto?
> hoc est quod unum est pro laboribus tantis.
> salue, o uenusta Sirmio, atque ero gaude
> gaudente, uosque, o Lydiae lacus undae,
> ridete quidquid est domi cachinnorum.

> *Sirmio—gem among islands and peninsulas—*
> *those that are set in limpid lake waters,*
> *those in vasty deep by Neptune in his other role—*
> *with what eagerness and joy my eye embraces you!*
> *Realization slowly comes that Thynia and Bithynia*
> *have been left behind, and I am safe to gaze at you.*
> *When is man happier than when troubles melt away?*
> *The mind lays down load. Tired from journey's labour*
> *I come to this my hearth and home,*
> *and take my rest in the bed I longed for.*
> *Only this can compensate for so much undertaken.*
> *Splendid Sirmio, I bid you greeting. Be joyful at*
> *your master's joy. Rippling Lydian lake,*
> *laugh with every resource of mirth you have.*

Note how sophistication and an obvious verbal artistry re-inforce the lyric impulse. The imagery of the opening lines is filled out with the playful solemnity of the invocation. The little recondite touches (the two Neptunes, the obscure dis-tinction between Thynia and Bithynia, the supposed Lydian origin of the Etruscans) contribute to the complex pleasure the lettered reader gets. Note the central reflective section which intervenes between the imagery of the first and last sections of the poem.

Though not dealing in emotions that are specially fresh or urgent, this is obviously a complicated, well-organized piece of poetic writing. The poem may fairly be called a lyric, pro-vided we use that label in the sense that Wordsworth gave it, or that modern poets give it when they attach it to poems compounded of reflection and a careful analysis of attitudes as much as of the impulse to song. It is emphatically not the simple song in praise of Sirmio that it is sometimes carelessly taken to be. The direct emotional incitement on which such a poem would depend is scrupulously avoided. The one epithet used directly of Sirmio, *uenusta* ('filled with charm, or grace'), a specifically non-poetic word that Catullus is fond of,[9] expresses a much more complex judgment than 'beautiful' or 'wonderful', and, because the word is normally applied to persons, not things, reinforces the hint of personification that the address of Sirmio implies. Moreover, the reasons that on this occasion made the poet specially aware of Sirmio's *uenustas* are carefully and soberly stated. It is these that pro-vide the real bond between poet and reader: what the poet communicates is not so much the description of a particular scene, but the unwinding of his thoughts in a situation we remember from comparable experiences of our own.

Some of the Lesbia poems are of this kind, for example Poem 2 ('Passer, deliciae meae puellae') or Poem 3 ('Lugete, o Veneres Cupidinesque'), to cite some of the most external and most deliberately poetic of the short pieces. Others of the Lesbia poems, for example Poem 8,

Miser Catulle, desinas ineptire,
et quod uides perisse perditum ducas.

You're being a fool, my poor Catullus. You must stop it and count as lost what you know is lost.

have a more private character—as though Catullus were trying to use the discipline of verse to see more clearly.[10]

Perhaps more significant is an intervening stage—satirical poems like the poem about the bridge at Colonia (Poem 17) and the poem about Harrius and his aitches (Poem 84). In these their status as poetry is beginning to preponderate over their purpose as invective or ridicule. Then there is Poem 97:

Non (ita me di ament) quicquam referre putaui,
utrumne os an culum olfacerem Aemilio.

Aemilius' mouth (the Gods us love!)
I didn't hesitate to class
as not, in smell, a scrap above
our friend Aemilius' arse.

Here, as in Poem 39, we have a poem filled with genial but outrageous obscenity where the very obscenity, perhaps, touches off a vein of poetic extravagance leading the poet away from the straight-out derision and abuse he originally intended. These poems, moreover, (Poem 97 especially) are far from negligible structurally. Poem 97 begins in a tone of measured, mock-disinterested statement, followed by a balanced couplet whose verbal polish is worthy of Ovid:

nilo mundius hoc, nihiloque immundius illud,
uerum etiam culus mundior et melior.

Then suddenly the poem flares up into a series of images the execution of which is as brilliant as their merciless fantasy is breathtaking. In Poem 39, by comparison, the *coup de massue* is perhaps too long delayed, and the limping iambic metre (however successful it may be in poems written on a higher level, e.g. Poems 8 and 31) is too flaccid a form for studied prosaic understatement. The elegiac couplet, on the other hand, has always a suggestion of measured reflection ideally suited to exploitation in stating every side of the problem Aemilius posed.

The gradation between the different levels of intent is, of course, continuous, and it would be foolish often to say of a particular poem that it is wholly lyric, wholly imaginative obscenity, or wholly abuse. The important thing is to keep at hand, as a serviceable critical tool, our awareness that these clearly different ingredients do enter into the poetry of Catullus in greatly varying proportions, the formula for their compounding in a given poem being dictated by the level of intent. Simply instead to lump together material so disparate as the Catullan collection, and to see everywhere a predominant lyricism, surely means stretching the term lyricism beyond useful limits.

When we come to look for reasons for this variation in intent, we should first of all remember it is far from certain that Catullus had in mind for all these poems the same sort of level of publication at any stage. Whether the poems were published at all by Catullus in the form in which we now have them is a question that is much argued about.[11] Even if we suppose the first group in our text (Poems 1-60) was arranged for publication by Catullus (this adequately explains the prefatory Poem 1, and the complicated metrical pattern of the arrangement), it seems hard to doubt that the degree to which the poet had publication in mind while writing varied enormously. An aspect of this question is studied in Chapter VI. The poems of Catullus differ probably in this respect from the Odes of Horace as much as the letters of Cicero from the letters of Pliny.

Another reason for the variation in intent is that, while Catullus' work as a whole is separated from that of Q. Lutatius Catulus and the epigrammatists by a very real poetic revolution, that revolution was still taking shape as Catullus wrote. Some of the short poems are still written in the spirit of the epigrammatists, and at that level of intent. These poems are separated by a gulf from those (the majority, perhaps) that spring clearly from a strongly felt, at times almost irresistible, impulse to expression.

If this notion of differing levels of intent is accepted, we must also face the likelihood that the long poems (63-8) represent Catullus' most sustained poetic endeavours. We may like them less than the best of his short poems, even though changing fashions in our own day may make us less blind to their real merits. We may discern in them many kinds of failure, but to try and dismiss all of them (except Poem 63) in such terms as 'a piece of hack-work written to order',[12] or 'episodes . . . strung together with a minimum of hasty narrative into an ill-assorted series',[13] even if these judgments sprang from a justifiable view of their poetic success, seems clearly a gross distortion of the poet's intentions. There can be little doubt that these compositions contain that part of his work that he intended to be taken most seriously. If they are also technical *tours de force*, that is because their author is anxious to show he is a serious artist, not, as might be imputed from the short poems, a poetic amateur.

The gradation of intent is clearest of all in the elegiac poems. Let us consider for the moment the short elegiac pieces only (Poems 69-116). The short elegiac poem was a recognized genre used to abuse a person addressed or as the vehicle for satirical comment on a person spoken of. It was compounded of wit, ingenuity and savage elegance of expression, rather than quality of imagery, complexity of diction, emotional depth or other more specially poetic qualities. The influence of Greek epigram is apparent. Moreover, as has been shown, we have here one of the streams of Roman poetic tradition that Catullus absorbed. In at least half of the fifty short elegiac pieces Catullus, taking over the genre presumably very much as he found it, works at a level which it is not very difficult to fix. We should not hesitate to fix it a good deal below what, by any strict standards, could be called serious poetry. Take Poem 113 for example:

Consule Pompeio primum duo, Cinna, solebant
    Maeciliam: facto consule nunc iterum
manserunt duo, sed creuerunt milia in unum
    singula. fecundum semen adulterio.

Fifteen years intervened between the two consulships of
Pompey, so that, in addition to the effect of mock solemnity
achieved by using the official formula for dating events, the
hint is dextrously, because obliquely, conveyed that Maecilia
is past her prime. The unexpressed viciousness is even greater
if Herescu is right in assuming that Maecilia is Pompey's
third wife, Mucia.[14]

In Pompey's first consulship, Cinna, Maecilia had
two lovers. Now he's consul for a second time.
The figure stays at 2, but they've grown a bit
and they're 2 thousand now. Fertile business, fornication.

This type of verse is almost completely devoid of imagery,
simile or metaphor. Except where the actual subject of the
epigram requires it (e.g. Mentula's estate in Poems 114 and
115), there is little mention of background or of concrete
things at all, so complete is the intellectualization of the
verse.

But at least a dozen of the fifty pieces climb well above this
level, though in different directions and as the result of dif-
ferent causes. This is not merely a judgment of quality,
though obviously of the epigrams which are epigrams pure
and simple some are more successful than others. But inter-
spersed with the epigrams pure and simple are pieces where
the short poem in elegiacs has been put to new uses, pieces of
which the most useful thing to say seems to be that they are
written at a different level. Sometimes it is mainly that the
quality of the emotion involved is superior, as in Poem 96:

Si quicquam mutis gratum acceptumue sepulcris
    accidere a nostro, Calue, dolore potest,
quo desiderio ueteres renouamus amores
    atque olim missas flemus amicitias,
certe non tanto mors immatura dolori est
    Quintiliae, quantum gaudet amore tuo.

The elaborate periodic sentence that somehow endows pro-
saic form with the thrill of poetry is such a feature of the
longer elegiac poems of Catullus that some effort should,
perhaps, be made to preserve it in translation:

> *If one result, Calvus, of our sorrowing is this*
> *that we bring some comfort or pleasure to unanswering*
> *   grave*
> *by that sense of longing we have when, thinking of them*
> *we loved, our tears start for friendships lost long ago;*
> *then surely the grief Quintilia feels at death too soon*
> *is less than the joy she feels that you love her still.*

Catullus is a master of this even-flowing, melancholy style—
compare this with Poem 76. Sometimes there is a violent and
deliberate contrast between this even flow of words and the
smouldering fury of what is being said—as in Poem 91.

A more familiar example is Poem 101 ('Multas per gentes
et multa per aequora uectus'), where, incidentally, it should
be noted how the imagery that most affects us in this splendid
poem—broad ocean, silent tomb, weeping poet—is mainly
indirectly suggested. Sometimes it is more the overall tone,
accompanied by a certain diminution of the intellectual snap,
that indicates that the poet is trying to do something more
ambitious, is trying to write on a higher or more worth-while
level than usual: Poems 84 ('Chommoda dicebat, si quando
commoda uellet') and 95 ('Zmyrna mei Cinnae nonam post
denique messem') are examples of 'epigrams' that are be-
ginning to show signs of having had more put into them than
epigrams can usually contain.

It is the Lesbia poems, of course, among these short elegiac
pieces that form the largest group. They also serve to warn
us against too rigid a classification. For many of the poems to
Lesbia (e.g. Poems 83, 92, 104) and most of the poems
addressed to his rivals (e.g. Poems 77, 91) might be regarded
simply as epigrams along with the rest. Even the famous
Poem 85

Odi et amo. quare id faciam, fortasse requiris?
nescio, sed fieri sentio et excrucior.

I hate her, and I love her. Do you ask the reason?
I cannot give you reason, but I feel the torment of it hap-
pening.

taken in isolation can hardly show the quickening introspection and the subtleties of self-analysis that Catullus learned to express more and more perfectly, adapting the antitheses of epigram to his special circumstances of heightened sensitivity and morbid vacillation. That this is the true character of these pieces, and that they are not the spontaneous cry-of-the-heart lyrics that they were once treated as being, has been increasingly recognized by scholars.[15]

Even more interesting in this respect than Poem 85 is Poem 82:

Quinti, si tibi uis oculos debere Catullum
   aut aliud si quid carius est oculis,
eripere ei noli, multo quod carius illi
   est oculis seu quid carius est oculis.

Quintius, shall Catullus feel he owes his eyes to you?
Or any other thing that's more to men than eyes?
Tear not then away what's more to him by far
than eyes. Or any thing that's more to men than eyes.

This is probably not a jealousy poem, as it is usually taken to be, but a poem addressed to a friend who is trying to help Catullus by freeing him from Lesbia's clutches and the misery that she is causing him: *eripere* almost certainly has the meaning that it has in Poem 76, line 20—as though some kind of surgical intervention were needed to free Catullus from his passion. (Cf. Propertius I. 1. 25 ff. This was the conventional role of the friend in the circle for which Catullus wrote.) 'Look,' says Catullus to his friend, 'do you want to put me in your debt?' Only he chooses the forceful colloquialism *oculos debere*, which means to owe life itself to someone. 'Do you want me to feel I owe you life itself?' That should be grati-

41

tude enough for being saved from the toils of a worthless mistress, as the affair appears from Quintius' point of view. But the phrase is not strong enough for Catullus and the hexameter, 'Do you want me to feel I owe you life itself?', flows on into the pentameter, 'Or whatever means more to men than life?' 'Well,' says Catullus, 'if you want me to feel that way, then—leave me alone. Don't try to tear her away from me, because (whatever the misery she causes me) she means more to me than life itself. Or, if there is something that means more to men than life, then she means still more to me than that.'

The achievement involved in sorting out this complicated pattern of thought and compressing it into four lines is almost bewildering. Catullus, however, manages not only to bring off this compression of thought and to express himself with an easy colloquialism that conceals the effort of compression, but to have space left for the haunting repetition in the last line of a whole phrase. The effect of the repetition is as though Catullus had realized he was putting things strongly; had stopped to ask himself if he really meant all he was saying; had decided he was sure he did mean it; and then reaffirmed his position with a calculatedly restrained emphasis. The first pentameter should be read with a rush of impatient excitement. That part of the second pentameter which contains the echo should be read slowly, in a tone of measured asseveration.

With these short poems in mind, it is instructive to compare the four-line epigram 75 ('Huc est mens deducta tua mea, Lesbia, culpa') and the fully rounded poem dealing with much the same situation and a similar attitude to it, but on the highest level, Poem 76 ('Siqua recordanti benefacta priora uoluptas'). Poems 70, 72, 87, 107, 109 are all attempts to explore the same personal dilemma in elegiac verse.[16] These are not only better poems than the epigrams pure and simple, they are the expression of a very different intent in the poet. In the former a relatively simple attitude is given the formal complexity of the elegiac epigram. In the latter the poet's effort is almost in the opposite direction: to utilize antithesis and formally juxtaposed statement in order to reduce a very complicated and deeply-felt nexus of feelings to disciplined and therefore expressible form. The long elegiac poems 66-8 represent another group with rather less personal involvement, and are certainly more deliberately poetic in tone. They are not yet successful elegies by Augustan standards, but many of the formal features of the new genre are apparent.[17]

The concept of levels of intent, once it is enunciated, seems probably so straightforward that it may be wondered why I have laboured it. It has been necessary to do so in order to combat the common view that there is something odd to be explained about Catullus as a poet—some psychic dichotomy that enabled him to write good poetry when he was not trying to, and which made him write bad poetry when he was. We must accustom ourselves, instead, to the idea that poetry was for Catullus the natural expression of his thoughts on all levels: on the occasions when he was poking fun at the human comedy; on those other occasions when, as Mr W. H. Auden puts it,

> *Rummaging into his living, the poet fetches*
> *The images out that hurt and connect;*

on those occasions, finally, when he was using all the resources of his talent to produce a work of art for which he hoped, as he said of Cinna's *Zmyrna*, that the 'grey-haired centuries to come will thumb its pages'.

CHAPTER IV

The Characteristics of the New Poetry

DID THE POETAE NOVI FORM A SCHOOL?

ONE piece of significant biographical information that emerges clearly from the Catullan poems is that their author was one of a group deeply interested in poetry. It is tantalizing to know so little of Catullus' relationships with his fellow-revolutionaries and his stature among them. The common view is that there existed a clearly recognized school of *poetae novi*, its most prominent members (after Catullus) being the orator Licinius Calvus and the minor politician Helvius Cinna. Cinna's *Zmyrna* is praised by Catullus in Poem 95, and the name of Calvus is linked by him with the discussion of the new poetry in two of the four poems where his name is mentioned—Poem 14, and especially Poem 50. Only small crumbs of their verse survive.[1] Others usually reckoned among the *poetae novi* and mentioned (probably) by Catullus are Cornificius, Valerius Cato and Furius Bibaculus. We have only a line or so of Cornificius and most likely nothing at all of Cato, though some attribute to him the *Lydia* and the *Dirae* of the Virgilian *Appendix*. Furius Bibaculus, however, is in some ways the best represented of the lot: in addition to a handful of fragments we have two complete poems, the longer extending to eight lines. Both poems unfortunately are confined by their subject, literary gossip, to a level of intent that makes them of little value as a guide to what Furius may have achieved when he was really trying. Catullus asks Cornificius for some verses to comfort him in Poem 38.[2] The Cato of Poem 56 could be Valerius Cato.[3] The Furius of Poems 11, 16, 23 and 26, also referred to in Poem 24, is likely to be Furius Bibaculus;[4] the usual interpretation of these poems, that Catullus is attacking this Furius, is perhaps the result of looking at them somewhat uncritically: exaggeratedly abusive language is not uncommon among friends, particularly if they are of Catullus' violent temperament, and there are hints in the Furius poems, and in other violent poems, that the abuse was not meant to wound—as it clearly was meant to in other poems, for example 28, 29, 47, or 59.[5]

Then there is the Caecilius of Poem 35 (not otherwise known); nor is it unreasonable to imagine that common interests in poetry, as well as in what Horace calls 'iuuenum curas et libera uina',[6] linked Catullus with the Flavius of Poem 6 (otherwise unknown); the Varus of Poem 10 (various candidates proposed); the book-loving Don Juan, Camerius, of Poems 55 and 58B (who may have been Cornificius' brother-in-law, but is otherwise unknown); and others besides. The only new poet of whose work fragments survive, but who is not named by Catullus, seems to be Ticidas. We need not, of course, doubt that many more existed of whom we know nothing.

Three passages of Cicero are customarily used to prove that the existence of a school was recognized by a contemporary. One of these (*T.D.* III. 45) has already been studied in another connection. The second comes from a letter written to Atticus (*Att.* VII. 2) at the end of the year 50 B.C. The letter begins:

Brundisium uenimus VII Kalend. Decembr. usi tua felicitate nauigandi; ita belle nobis

Flauit ab Epiro lenissimus Onchesmites.

Hunc σπονδειάζοντα si cui uoles τῶν νεωτέρων pro tuo uendito.

The term 'neoteric', often applied by modern scholars to the new poets, owes its origin to this passage. The neoteric flavour of Cicero's hexameter is usually supposed to reside only in the spondaic fifth foot, but the line has a lot of the ring of Catullus' Poem 64 about it stylistically, as well as metrically. The five-word hexameter is frequent in Poem 64. So, too, is the trick of the learned name: *Onchesmites* is the wind that

blew from Onchesmus in Epirus towards Italy (Horace's
Iapyx).[7] Compare (on all these points) line 28 of Poem 64:

tene Thetis tenuit pulcerrima Nereine.

Both here and in line 395 the epithet chosen by Catullus
(*Nereine* may not be right) is so obscure that the manuscript
tradition has been confused.

The third quotation contains another term much used by
modern critics, *poetae novi*. It deals with the dropping by
these poets of the old licence that allowed a final 's' before an
initial consonant to be disregarded metrically:

> Quin etiam, quod iam subrusticum uidetur, olim autem
> politius, eorum uerborum, quorum eaedem erant postremae
> duae litterae quae sunt in *optimus*, postremam litteram
> detrahebant, nisi uocalis insequebatur. Ita non erat ea
> offensio in uersibus quam nunc fugiunt poetae noui. Sic
> enim loquebamur:
>
> > qui est omnibu' princeps
>
> non *omnibus princeps*, et:
>
> > uita illa dignu' locoque
>
> non *dignus*.[8]

Cicero need not, of course, be pointing to anything more than
a difference in practice between contemporary poets and older
poets in general. This view is consistent with Cicero's own
practice, as far as we can judge from the fragments of his
verse. The device occurs only in his earliest verse. He seems
therefore to have already abandoned it before Catullus be-
gan writing.[9] Any special colour that we read into the phrase
poetae novi can only come therefore from our associating this
passage with the other two.

The view that a school existed has been strongly attacked.[10]
It seems that whether there was a clear-cut 'school', and
whether its members were commonly referred to as the
poetae novi or the *neoteri*, are matters that must, at least,
remain in doubt. (We need not for that reason avoid the con-

venient term *poetae novi* which modern use has made fami-
liar.) It should be noted, incidentally, that none of the quota-
tions from Cicero comes from a work written during Catullus'
lifetime. The earliest (the letter to Atticus) was probably
written several years after Catullus' death, and the other two
are four to five years later still. The existence of a clear-cut
Catullan school in the formative years of Virgil and Horace
is, of course, an exciting possibility and fits in well enough
with the view that Calvus (who died, probably, in 47 B.C.)
and Cinna (who was assassinated, probably, in 44 B.C.) were
members of it. Our concern here, however, must be not with
the state of affairs in the middle forties, but with a period
twenty to twenty-five years earlier, at the outbreak of the
Catullan revolution.

Even if the existence of some sort of school is admitted,
there is nothing to indicate that Catullus was its head. His
relationship in terms of leader and disciple to the poets he
names is undeterminable. Some hold the leader was Valerius
Cato, basing their view on a passage in Suetonius, where Cato
is called *peridoneus praeceptor* and an epigram quoted which
is usually attributed to Furius Bibaculus, where Cato is
clearly regarded as an authority on poetry, though it is not
clear whether in the phrase 'solus legit ac facit poetas' *facit*
means 'rightly evaluates' or 'establishes the reputation of'.[11]
Valerius Cato is lavishly praised by other *poetae novi*,[12] but,
the *Lydia* and the *Dirae* apart, nothing survives to test their
judgments. Even if he wrote little of any worth, this would
not be the only instance known of a critic directing tyran-
nically a new poetic movement, though himself an indifferent
poet.

Still less determinable is to what extent these shadowy
figures took their poetry seriously. Did their work possess
only the elegant triviality of Laevius, or was it pervaded with
the new spiritual atmosphere that wrenched the *nugae* away
from the level of scholarly persiflage and their longer poems
from the level of erudite dullness up to the level of front-
rank poetry?

What should be incontestable (though it has been contested) is that Catullus wrote, and discussed with other poets in poems that are extant (e.g. Poems 14, 22, 35, 36, 50, 65, 95, 116), a kind of poetry that had certain highly novel overall features. Wrongheadedness and formalism have in the past sometimes obscured this truth, though it is today more generally admitted. Catullus and his friends must, of course, have had some realization of where they were heading, though, once again, the distant critic may have a clearer view of the contours of the terrain—clearer certainly than many contemporaries, clearer perhaps than the poets had themselves.

Despite these unresolvable uncertainties, Catullus' own poems make it clear that he was one of a group of poets who shared confidences, aspirations and ideas about poetry and literary criticism. It is also clear that these ideas had a permanent influence on Roman poetry. Inevitably we must try to guess at their shape from the surviving work of the one poet about whose poetry we really know anything. It is difficult to make any sure critical assessment of the surviving fragments of the other new poets, but there is a good deal in them all the same to suggest that, in both tone and style, they were close to Catullus.

THE POETRY OF YOUTH AND REACTION

Beginning a recent discussion on Catullus, a French scholar, J. Bayet,[13] sets out from an overall generalization about the contours of the new movement (as we should, perhaps, call it in order to avoid the word 'school'). It was, he says, 'un phénomène de jeunesse. . . . Des jeunes gens, peu nombreux, instruits, curieux, . . . complices . . . contre la génération précédente, celle de Cicéron'. The first factor—youth with its independence, its recklessness, its singleness in enthusiasm —emerges clearly from the poems.[14] Catullus himself tells us he had just assumed the toga of manhood when his first experiences of love came—and he began writing:[15]

tempore quo primum uestis mihi tradita pura est,
    iucundum cum aetas florida uer ageret,
multa satis lusi: non est dea nescia nostri,
    quae dulcem curis miscet amaritiem.

(Poem 68, 15-18)

There was the time when I had just been given my plain
  white toga.
I was the age to flower with the joy of spring.
I took my full share of life's fun. My name is well known
  to the goddess
who concocts the bitter-sweet anguish of love.

Bayet's second point, that the Catullan movement was a movement opposed to Cicero and his generation, may be restated more elaborately. Because of Cicero's long life and Catullus' short one, we tend to lose sight of the fact that the poet was something like twenty to twenty-five years younger than the orator. In terms of poetic tradition, it is the representatives of the epic-tragic stream that Cicero valued highest among Roman poets and it was their style he had himself followed and in some technical matters improved. Cicero is sometimes supposed to have passed through a neoteric phase himself. It is certainly possible, though we may suspect he was too old before the movement began. Aratus (whom Cicero translated) was an Alexandrian, but an interest in his learned didactic poetry did not necessarily make Cicero an adherent of the new movement taking shape in Rome in Cicero's own time. If we look at the Catullans in terms of personalities, then Bayet is clearly right. But we should remember that the enmities and friendships of good poets are more transitory than their poetry. If, therefore, we try to think instead in terms of the evolution of the Roman poetic tradition, we should perhaps say the generation of Cicero piaced highest the epic-tragic stream of that tradition, whereas Catullus represents a fusion of the three streams of tradition that reached him.

THE POETRY OF CATULLUS: ITS UNDERLYING UNITY

But it is time we passed from the poets themselves and their attitudes to an examination of some of the distinctive qualities of what they wrote. In the previous chapter, I tried to show the shallowness of the view that there are two Catulluses ('learned' and 'lyric'), and to substitute for that notion the notion of levels of poetic intent. The notion of levels of intent, however, if left unqualified, tends to suggest a disintegrated, discontinuous view of Catullus' poetry. We need a formula to tune our thinking, to give us some feeling for what all their new poetry had in common and what was new in it. We can get this, perhaps, by lifting a phrase from a recent study of a single poem. J.-P. Boucher,[16] seeking such a formula in order to integrate Poem 64 with the remainder of Catullus' work, calls it the kind of poetry where 'la sensibilité du poète est engagée'. Catullus is not a professional poet or a dilettante, he says, but a writer whose personal reactions are involved in the story he tells in Poem 64, and it is these reactions that dictate the whole layout of the poem. It is not simply that Catullus lets us feel he cares about Ariadne. We are made constantly to feel the *presence* of the poet by the way in which he directs the story, altering its tempo, imposing on stylized ancient legend an ironical overlay of modern realistic detail, giving the poem constantly the imprint of his own personality.

This personal involvement of the poet is something new that the Roman temperament brought to ancient poetry at this stage. The Greeks were capable of the acutest analysis of passion and able to frame it in high poetry. The Hellenistic poets exploited deliberately and obviously clever arrangement and layout of a poem. But about both ages of Greek literature there was always something external and intellectual. Even when Hellenistic poets made usual the fashion of writing in the first person, a coldness, a withholding of self persisted.[17] Any wholesale condemnation of Greek literature for its impersonal character would obviously be absurd. It results in some departments of literature in a nobility and an objective purity the Romans never matched. Its limitations only appear when Hellenistic poets start writing of themselves.

One notices the same intrusion of the personal when one compares Roman sculpture with Greek. Catullus, like Keats, was a barbarian who so transformed the raw material of his own life in his poetry that it attained heroic stature, and who contrariwise experienced the excitement of personal involvement in re-creating what a modern poet has called—approvingly

legends that strut in verses out of the past,[18]

because the stuff of legend has an organized tension about it that the rawer material of contemporary life seems to the poet to lack.

Interaction between the elements of self and legend is constant. The long poems are vitalized by this feeling of participation, the short poems are often thereby made to soar from the level of conversation improved upon (when urbanity and sophistication are the predominant qualities of the verse) to the level of very real poetry by a single evocative phrase. This need not involve straightout employment of mythological material—rare in Catullus, compared with the elegiac poets. As an example of how the unreal, romantic world surges up at the slightest touch, consider the effect of the two words *candida puella* in Poem 13:

> Cenabis bene, mi Fabulle, apud me
> paucis, si tibi di fauent, diebus,
> si tecum attuleris bonam atque magnam
> cenam, non sine candida puella
> et uino et sale et omnibus cachinnis.

You'll dine in style, dear Fabullus, when you come to me,
any day now, if the gods are kind to you.
So long as you bring a good square meal along as well.
And don't forget some radiant creature—
and a bottle of wine, some salt and a full supply of stories.

Into the narrow world of this elegantly worded invitation, in which pure form is at once the stimulus of genius and the justification of the poem as literature,[19] is suddenly thrust the vision, heavy with overtones, of the radiant beauty of an unknown girl. Compare Catullus' use of the same word, applied to a woman, in Poem 35, 8, and especially Poem 68, 70 (*mea candida diua*), where he chooses this epithet at the moment when he likens his mistress to a goddess.[20]

Consider also how much is built into Poem 7 while answering the question 'How many kisses are enough?' The question could have been treated on a purely intellectual plane of metaphysical wit—as it would have been if, for example, the opening two lines of Poem 7 had been followed by lines 7-13 of Poem 5, and that poem deprived of its lyrical overtones by removing lines 3-5. We should then have a poem like this:

> Quaeris, quot mihi basiationes
> tuae, Lesbia, sint satis superque. (Poem 7, 1-2)
> da mi basia mille, deinde centum,
> dein mille altera, dein secunda centum,
> deinde usque altera mille, deinde centum.
> dein, cum milia multa fecerimus,
> conturbabimus illa, ne sciamus,
> aut ne quis malus inuidere possit,
> cum tantum sciat esse basiorum. (Poem 5, 7-13.)

> *You ask me, Lesbia, how many kisses it will take*
> *to make me really satisfied.*
> *Give me a thousand kisses, followed by a hundred;*
> *another thousand then, and a second hundred.*
> *Then a further thousand, plus a hundred.*
> *Finally, when we've made it many thousands,*
> *please muddle all the accounts and forget the total.*
> *Then no nosey nasty person will be able to be envious*
> *through knowledge of such heavy transacting in kisses.*[21]

This combination of the more purely intellectual parts of two poems would have given us a perfectly acceptable non-lyric, non-imaginative epigram. Instead in Poem 7 we have:

Quaeris, quot mihi basiationes
tuae, Lesbia, sint satis superque.
quam magnus numerus Libyssae harenae
lasarpiciferis iacet Cyrenis
oraclum Iouis inter aestuosi
et Batti ueteris sacrum sepulcrum;
aut quam sidera multa, cum tacet nox,
furtiuos hominum uident amores:
tam te basia multa basiare
uesano satis et super Catullo est,
quae nec pernumerare curiosi
possint nec mala fascinare lingua.

You ask me, Lesbia, how many kisses it will take
to make me really satisfied.
As many as the sands of Libya's desert
that lies round Cyrene where the silfium grows,
stretching between the oracle of sweltering Jove
and the holy tomb of Battus long ago departed.
Or as many as the stars that in night's quiet
look down on us mortals stealing love.
That is the total of the kisses that will make
your passionate Catullus really satisfied.
A sum like that the nosey couldn't reckon up,
or evil tongues weave spells around.

The poem is laden with the qualities that controlled imagi-
nation can impart. Jove's ancient shrine in the sweltering
desert. The magic of night that Virgil re-caught in his

ibant obscuri sola sub nocte per umbram.

But night's magic is always easily evoked and it would have
been a blemish in so short a poem to use as a second image of
countless number a thing so commonplace—if it had not been
given special appropriateness. The lyric and imaginative im-
pulse is strengthened, therefore, by our sharing with the poet
the thrill of an ironical reference to the poet's own *furtiuus*
amor with Lesbia.[22]

The term *controlled lyricism* may serve to label what is going on in this poem and others like it (for example, Poem 31, discussed in the previous chapter). The lyrical impulse is tightened by an intellectual awareness of significance and proportion, which controls and organizes what is said. Even in the poems of completest surrender to emotion we can have the feeling that Catullus is aware of the course the poem must take—if it is to remain the sort of poem this tension between intellect and emotion best produces. Contrast the surrender to the lyric impulse in Tibullus and his uncritical acceptance of emotion. Poetry can be written the Tibullan way, too, but its characteristic will be charm rather than strength. In Horace and Ovid, on the other hand, the intellect has a sort of non-*engagé* effect, framing the emotional vignette that each ode or elegy constitutes, suggesting a judgment (often, in Horace, of a scene involving others and not, on the surface, personal at all) and a point of view.

This is perhaps the point for a word about 'sincerity'. The common view rightly stresses the sincerity of Catullus' poetry, but tends to confuse poetic sincerity with autobiographical truth. The following judgment on poetry, for example, would, I think, still win ready acceptance among many students of classical literature, not only for the eloquence with which it is expressed:

the Lesbia cycle cannot be paralleled in ancient literature for sincerity of passion, passing through all the stages of joyous contentment, growing distrust, and wild despair to the poignant adieu of the disillusioned lover.[23]

Few modern literary critics, however, would accept the doctrine of *Dichtung und Wahrheit* in so ingenuous a form. They would deny that sincerity of this sort is vital to good poetry. And, conversely, that Catullus' poetry must be good because it seems to record authentic experience. Sincerity, like other forms of emotion, is no more than an ingredient of poetry, essential to securing the temperature of fusion of the poet's raw material into poetry. It is at best a poor criterion of quality, and its relationship to factual truth is complicated.[24]

A measure of *insincerity* even is not incompatible with good poetry, though in Roman poetry we have to wait till Horace for the studied exploitation of attitudes so complex in the poet to his subject-matter.

METRE AND STRUCTURE

Another characteristic of the new poetry is its exploitation of the possibilities of metrical variety. The course of the old Roman tradition here has already been indicated, from the *cantica* of Plautus through the polymetric *nugae* of Laevius. In the *poetae novi* this is first and foremost a matter of intense interest in metrical experiment. The excitement it could produce in Catullus is clear from Poem 50:

> Hesterno, Licini, die otiosi
> multum lusimus in meis tabellis,
> ut conuenerat esse delicatos:
> scribens uersiculos uterque nostrum
> ludebat numero modo hoc modo illoc,
> reddens mutua per iocum atque uinum.
> atque illinc abii tuo lepore
> incensus, Licini, facetiisque,
> ut nec me miserum cibus iuuaret
> nec somnus tegeret quiete ocellos,
> sed toto indomitus furore lecto
> uersarer, cupiens uidere lucem,
> ut tecum loquerer simulque ut essem.
> at defessa labore membra postquam
> semimortua lectulo iacebant,
> hoc, iucunde, tibi poema feci,
> ex quo perspiceres meum dolorem.
> nunc audax caue sis, precesque nostras,
> oramus, caue despuas, ocelle,
> ne poenas Nemesis reposcat a te.
> est uehemens dea: laedere hanc caueto.

The poem ends with an elaborately pathetic entreaty for another meeting. Licinius Calvus is to be supposed as receiving the poem first thing the next morning. This becomes clearer if we change the past tenses in the second half to presents: it was common in Latin letters for the writer to adopt in matters of time the standpoint of the recipient. Indeed 'yesterday' in the first line, by our conventions, should perhaps be 'today', though we may keep 'yesterday' for convenience and assume the poem was written after midnight. Two further points should be noted: the way in which Catullus consciously suggests the tone of a love-letter, even in details of vocabulary (e.g. *miserum; dolorem*)[25] in order to convey an intellectual or artistic excitement that is as acute as sensual excitement; and the degree to which this ostensibly spontaneous poem has been arranged for publication, by sketching in the circumstances in the opening lines—Calvus did not need to be told what Catullus tells him.[26] The poem is more complex than might at first appear.

How well spent, Licinius, the idle hours of yesterday!
I'd my notebook with me and we had glorious fun,
sophisticated by arrangement.
Each of us took his turn at versifying,
gaily experimenting with metre after metre,
vying with the other while we joked and drank.
I left for home, fascinated,
Licinius, by the elegance of your wit.
My dinner gave me no comfort. I was in a torment.
Nor could sleep lid my eyes or bring me rest.
Gripped by excitement I cannot tame, I've been tossing
all around my bed, impatient for the day,
hoping we can be together and I can talk with you.
Finally, exhausted with fatigue, extended
on my bed, half-way now to death,
I've made, dear friend, this poem for you,
so you can understand the torture I've been through.
Take care, please, do not be foolhardy;
do not say No, dearest friend, to my request,
lest avenging Nemesis exact her retribution.
Don't provoke the goddess. She can be violent.

The fascination that metrical problems have for front-rank poets is hard, perhaps, for those of us who are not poets to understand. We have still to resist a tendency to equate interest in technique with inferior genius—a carry-over of the romantic doctrine of lyrical inspiration. Though, rather curiously, it is more fashionable to disparage Horace for a preoccupation with metre than Catullus. Yet the importance attributed to metre by leading poets today is easy to gather from their readiness to discuss this and other aspects of technique, and from the confessions poets occasionally make to us about their methods of composition.[27] In Roman literature these enthusiasms for technique were novel. The old craftsman-poet was conservative and rightly so, because cleverness was not his business. Cleverness that went beyond the very occasional special effect would thrust the personality of the artist into the work of art, and in epic and tragedy the artist should remain anonymous.

All the same, the way in which the short poems of Catullus fall into two groups is remarkable: Poems 1 to 60 are written *numero modo hoc modo illoc*, but Poems 69 to 116 are all in elegiacs. As far as we can tell, Catullus practised the two genres simultaneously, not at any stage abandoning either for the other as his successors did: the polymetric poems prepared the way for the *Epodes* and the *Odes* of Horace, the elegiac poems for Augustan elegy. In Catullus, the subject-matter of both genres is often the same, though the treatment of it is usually very different, except at the lowest level of intent where an abusive epigram in hendecasyllabics may not differ greatly from an epigram in elegiacs. On the higher levels of composition, the polymetric poems display greater surges of emotion, more spontaneous writing we may say—provided by spontaneous we mean an effect of art, and do not suppose spontaneity to exclude long preparation or structural complexity. The elegiacs are less exuberant in their wording, though they often display a restrained ferocity. There are elements of tradition latent in this distinction, though not enough to make it clear why Catullus chose to develop the distinction so sharply.

Coupled with metrical experiment is a new attention to structural problems. In epic poetry the canvas is so vast that the quality of the structure is less important. In the drama, and in the didactic poetry of Lucretius, there is necessarily an initial layout of the material, but nothing approaching the structural tightness that a good short poem must have. In Catullus, the qualities of concision and slickness are so apparent that it is hardly necessary to quote examples from the short poems. Even in the longest poems, e.g. 64 and 68, there is a new attention not only to overall structure, but, instead of a loose string of purple passages, an effect of carefully calculated contrast (e.g. in Poem 64 between description of scene and direct speech), as well as studied exploitation of the unexpected angle and of the diversity of layout in description, extremely detailed description contrasting sharply with succinct résumé.[28] In structure, too, the polymetric poems and the elegiac poems differ, the latter displaying a more closely-knit logical sequence of thought, as opposed to the cyclic effect that we get often in the polymetric poems, where a single idea is enunciated, expanded, and then reiterated.[29]

LANGUAGE

With the new poets came a remarkable renovation in the language of Roman poetry. The language of serious poetry, that of epic and tragedy, had really changed very little since the days of Ennius. An effective poetic style (and Ennius' was that) tends, once formed, to persist until its remoteness from living language deprives it of vitality to a degree that is felt to be intolerable and to make it unfit for the effective expression of any sincerely felt emotion.

Differences between the two kinds of poetic language are obvious. Though of course there are common features. Catullus keeps, for example, in his more serious writing (in Poems 63 and 64, in the more seriously intended elegies) to that rugged, highly alliterative style which goes back to the very origins of Roman poetry. Unfortunately, apart from studies of points of detail, little has been done to investigate the differences adequately—or the relationship of epic language and Catullan language to other Roman poetic styles.[30] Moreover, the usual approach is based on an ancient grammatical tradition that treats the language of poetry as merely the vehicle of the sense—as though there existed first a body of material to be communicated which is then wrapped in a garb of poetic language. Any good poetry is more than this sort of product of versifying ideas. Such an approach becomes, however, hopeless when we have to deal with the intensely cohering compositions of the *poetae novi*, where every detail of word, sound and metre, and the organization of these into an integrated whole, are active constituents of the poetry. Though this is almost a commonplace of modern literary criticism,[31] it is perhaps worth reiteration here.

The new climate in literary criticism is, of course, the outcome of changes in the way poetry has been written in our time. The nature of the phenomenon with which we have to deal in Catullus can be more readily understood, therefore, today than fifty years ago as a result of the comparable renewal that we have seen in the language of poetry in our own literature. The similarity between the two movements is at least sufficient to make it worth taking advantage of the acuter feeling we necessarily possess for our own language in order to get some feeling for what happened with the *poetae novi*.

The source of these renovations when they occur is the living, everyday language. In Roman literature, the elements of a style drawing upon everyday speech already existed in the comic-satiric stream of tradition. What the *poetae novi* had to do was to adapt the racy directness of speech so that it could be used for serious poetry. The degree of adaptation depended on the level of poetic intent. The colloquialism of Catullus is, of course, well recognized by scholars, though it is seldom adequately represented by Catullus' many translators in recent years.[32] Indeed the gulf that separates the *poetae novi* from their Alexandrian 'models' is perhaps deepest here. The diction of Hellenistic poetry is, by comparison, an odd jumble of worn, pretentious literary archaism. Despite the many technical achievements of that brilliant movement, we see here a symptom of disease, the result of making poetry in a kind of literary laboratory.

Of course, even at the lowest levels of intent the new poetry, like the dialogue of Oscar Wilde's comedies, contains a great deal of artistic improvement upon the conversation of the most brilliantly sophisticated set. In Catullus, the language of conversation is improved upon in two directions. Firstly, as in Wilde, by a heightened tension, giving the appearance, still, of naturalness, but bringing about a sustained brilliance which is the effect of art. Quite apart from metre, we may be sure the *poetae novi* never talked in this way. This improvement upon conversation is so straightforward we need not do more than mention it, as a warning against those who put the case for colloquialism too simply. It cannot, alone, make poetry out of speech. If we are to get the right feeling for Catullus, we must grasp a second way in which his language (despite its colloquial raciness), by a subtle infiltration of the unobtrusively archaic, the unusual and even the exotic, assumes the evident tone, the solemnity almost, that serious poetry requires. Again, a look at modern poetry may help us to get our bearings. Let us take Robert Graves's poem 'The Cool Web' as an illustration of one kind of poetic language, concentrating our attention on that aspect only:

> *Children are dumb to say how hot the day is,*
> *How hot the scent is of the summer rose,*
> *How dreadful the black wastes of evening sky,*
> *How dreadful the tall soldiers drumming by.*
>
> *But we have speech, to chill the angry day,*
> *And speech, to dull the rose's cruel scent.*
> *We spell away the overhanging night,*
> *We spell away the soldiers and the fright.*
>
> *There's a cool web of language winds us in,*
> *Retreat from too much joy or too much fear:*
> *We grow sea-green at last and coldly die*
> *In brininess and volubility.*

But if we let our tongues lose self-possession,
Throwing off language and its watery clasp
Before our death, instead of when death comes,
Facing the wide glare of the children's day,
Facing the rose, the dark sky and the drums,
We shall go mad no doubt and die that way.

There is hardly a detail in this poem of which we could say that it belonged to literature only and not to living language. Even the omission of the relative pronoun in the first line of the third stanza occurs in colloquial language, in addition to its regional and archaic overtones. There are whole lines that we might without difficulty use in conversation. Yet, quite apart from the obvious structural qualities of the poem: the incantatory effect, for example, of the patterns of repetition (remember what prominent features anaphora and circular composition are of Catullan style); quite apart from the special exploitation of certain words (the deliberate ambiguity of 'spell' for example, the personifying effect of applying the epithet 'cruel' to a rose's scent, or the unusual syntax of 'dumb to say'); apart from all these apparent devices, the poem is pervaded by both a tightness of tone and a solemnity that make it quite unlike prose. And this is a comparatively neutral example, because we have chosen a poem which contains no dialogue.

Stylistic comparisons between any modern poet and an ancient one should not be pushed too far, though most of the devices in this poem could, I think, be paralleled from Catullus. What we want from Graves's poem is a general impression of style to tune our reactions to Catullus. Almost any Catullan poem that is more than a few lines long can make us feel the power a comparable *crispness* of diction possesses to create the atmosphere of poetry. The effect is discreetly heightened by the unusual turn of phrase or word. The alternation of colloquialism and elaborate polysyllable should particularly be noted.

The most instructive poems are those whose raw material

(that which becomes the subject-matter when the poem has been made) provides no obvious poetic impulse. Consider what Catullus does with the situation he deals with in Poem 6:

> Flaui, delicias tuas Catullo,
> ni sint illepidae atque inelegantes,
> uelles dicere nec tacere posses.
> uerum nescio quid febriculosi
> scorti diligis: hoc pudet fateri.
> nam te non uiduas iacere noctes
> nequiquam tacitum cubile clamat
> sertis ac Syrio fragrans oliuo,
> puluinusque peraeque et hic et ille
> attritus, tremulique quassa lecti
> argutatio inambulatioque.
> nam nil stupra ualet, nihil tacere.
> cur? non tam latera ecfututa pandas,
> ni tu quid facias ineptiarum.
> quare, quidquid habes boni malique,
> dic nobis. uolo te ac tuos amores
> ad caelum lepido uocare uersu.

The situation is a stock one—the young man who won't produce his girl for inspection.[33] Smartness and sophistication are the key-notes of the poem.

> *Flavius, you've a sweetheart, but she must*
> *be just a bit uncouth, not entirely U perhaps,*
> *or you'd want to talk of her, couldn't help it even.*
> *I expect it's some feverish little baggage*
> *that you're in love with, and ashamed of owning up.*
> *They're no celibate nights you're passing. Your room,*
> *though tongueless, shrieks its testimony just the same.*
> *All those flowers, that oily Syrian scent,*
> *those pillows crumpled just as much on either side,*
> *that rickety bed, so knocked about it emits*
> *falsetto creaks as it wanders round the room.*
> *Not the slightest use refusing to talk.*

Why, you're an obvious case of
There must be funny business ƒ
So tell us who she is you've got-
or bad. I want to poeticize your love .
and raise you to the sky in polished verse.

To confine ourselves to diction: consider the contra
the striking polysyllables *febriculosi* (with a delibera
coarse word juxtaposed),[34] *argutatio, inambulatio* (two ex-
travagant abstract nouns that make up a line between them)
and that of the personification implied by *clamat* or *uiduas.*
Exuberant fantasy is allowed to run its delicious course, and
then at the end the poem wheels round on to a more seriously
poetic note: there is perhaps the stuff of poetry in this affair
between Flavius and his mistress, and Catullus is eager to
exploit it.

The atmosphere of a poem like this is difficult to create and
Catullus is not always successful in his choice of language.
Contrast the opening half of Poem 39:

> Egnatius, quod candidos habet dentes,
> renidet usque quaque. si ad rei uentum est
> subsellium, cum orator excitat fletum,
> renidet ille; si ad pii rogum fili
> lugetur, orba cum flet unicum mater,
> renidet ille. quidquid est, ubicumque est,
> quodcumque agit, renidet: hunc habet morbum,
> neque elegantem, ut arbitror, neque urbanum.

Egnatius has got teeth that are shining white, and so he
* breaks*
on every conceivable occasion into a flashing grin. The
* prisoner's*
in the dock. His counsel's working at our tears. Egnatius
breaks into a flashing grin. Or at a funeral: grief on every
* side*
the mother who's bereaved laments her model son. Egna-
* tius*

eaks into a flashing grin. On every conceivable occasion,
o matter what he's doing, that flashing grin. It's a com-
plaint he suffers from
and one that's neither smart, I think, nor sophisticated.

Here the attempt to transform prose statement by the struc-
tural force of repetition (e.g. the *renidet ille*, repeated at the
same position in the line, the parallel *cum* clauses) somehow
fails.

It is this effect which I have been calling *crispness* (to de-
note something that is fairly evident in illustration, but hard
to analyse) that Havelock felt, perhaps, when he called these
poems 'lyrical'. But even taken in this way, that term narrows
too much the range of tone that we find in Catullus. Consider
Poem 10: here the same crispness of language gives life to
a poem where anything approaching emotional outburst is
carefully held in check in order to achieve a mixture of narra-
tive and urbane comment that was to prepare the way for the
best hexameter writing of Horace. On the other hand, dis-
creetly strengthened with some of the traditional devices of
poetry, it contributes to the success of Poems 63 and 64. Even
in these long narrative poems, the straightout inflation of
rhetoric and the artificial intensity of rhetoric are avoided—
except in the set speeches (a prominent feature of both
poems), which acquire thereby a deliberately archaic, 'epic'
tone with which the mannered slickness of the narrative sec-
tions is set in calculated contrast. Consider this passage of
Poem 63:

> ita de quiete molli rapida sine rabie
> simul ipsa pectore Attis sua facta recoluit,
> liquidaque mente uidit sine quis ubique foret,
> animo aestuante rusum reditum ad uada tetulit.
> ibi maria uasta uisens lacrimantibus oculis,
> patriam allocuta maestast ita uoce miseriter.
> 'patria o mei creatrix, patria o mea genetrix . . .
> ubinam aut quibus locis te positam, patria, reor?'

> (Poem 63, 44-50, 55)

The narrative opening of this section, unadorned by tradi-
tional rhetorical devices other than alliteration, but drawing
vigour from forceful, unconventional words, contrasts with
the loose declamatory style of Attis' speech, which is almost
a pastiche of tragic style:

Then, when after soft repose, free from madness' grasp,
Attis himself in mind reviewed his situation,
and with intellect cleared perceived where he was and what
*   he lacked,*
thought once more seething he returned to the water's
*   edge,*
and scanning with tear-brimmed eyes the ocean's vast
*   extent,*
pitifully addressed with sorrowing voice his native land:
'O land where I was conceived, land where I was born . . .
where, in what place, shall I think you situate?'

A detailed analysis of Catullan language cannot, however,
be attempted here, though there is urgent need both for
intensive research into points of language that have never
been looked at, and for bringing together the studies of de-
tail that have been made, in order to give meaning to dry
lists of words and points of syntax in terms of what poets
really do. It is obviously not enough, for example, to say that
diminutives are a feature of Catullus' style and give a list of
them. It is still not enough to say their effect is colloquial.
Take Poem 64, line 131:

frigidulos udo singultus ore cientem

with tearful face summoning chilly sobs
or line 316:

laneaque aridulis haerebant morsa labellis
and from the dried-up lips hung wisps of wool, bitten off.

In these contexts the diminutives have the power both to
create pathos and to heighten the interpenetration of legend
and reality that we have spoken of earlier.

The archaism of Catullus has been sometimes exaggerated. The language of his contemporary Lucretius is much more deeply penetrated with archaism. Nevertheless, archaic touches exist, producing, among other effects, simplicity and solemnity. And archaism is, of course, a constant device in Poems 63 and 64, poems whose strength comes largely from a basic archaism and non-naturalism of tone (emphasized by static, heavily detailed pictures: e.g. Poem 64, 52-70) given a fresh subtlety by gentle but conscious touches of ironical realism.[35]

A more complicated element of Catullan language is the employment of Greek words and constructions. Often Greek words (e.g. *mnemosynum, pathicus, catagraphus,* and, probably, *strophium*) are part of the sophisticated slang of the circle of the *poetae novi*.[36] An example of a more complicated trick (the sort of thing we might associate more with Virgil than Catullus) is given by Ronconi:[37]

> nutricum tenus exstantes e gurgite cano
>
> (Poem 64, 18)

In this line, the use of *nutrix* for *mamma* probably depends on the reader's knowing that a Greek word for *nutrix* also means *mamma*.

Lastly, we may mention the Graecisms of syntax: the use of an accusative after a passive participle, for example,

> non contectá léui uelatum pectus amictu,
> non tereti strophio lactentis uincta papillas
>
> (Poem 64, 64-5)

giving an effect that is novel, that draws upon the hearer's erudition. The sense in which this construction may be called a Graecism needs to be precisely stated. It should be obvious that a writer of any skill will not simply import from another language a wholly alien piece of syntactical idiom. The requirements are best met stylistically when the alien construction is comprehensible, offers positive advantage (freshness, concision), and is only just not normal syntax. For example, 'From the worth-nothing that he was he is become a personage' is a series of syntactical Gallicisms in English obvious to those who know French ('Du vaurien qu'il était, il est devenu un personnage'), but offering stylistic possibilities whether this is recognized or not; whereas, say, 'I demanded of him how it did itself that this should be arrived' completely lacks these possibilities of stylistic exploitation. The same conditions apply to the stylistic exploitation of Greek syntax in Latin. In the case of the example quoted: there are traces of a middle past participle with a direct object in Latin from early times, just enough for the Greek construction to be understood and felt as a kind of Latin, unusual but effective. It therefore becomes possible to exploit the much greater use made in Greek of this construction and its affinity with the accusative of respect in Greek, a construction that is not Latin at all.

Another example from Catullus is his use of *ut* with the subjunctive in imitation of Greek ὡς, for example:[38]

> sed quid ego a primo digressus carmine plura
> commemorem, *ut* linquens genitoris filia uultum,
> *ut* consanguineae complexum, *ut* denique matris,
> quae misera in gnata deperdita laetabatur,
> omnibus his Thesei dulcem praeoptarit amorem:
> aut *ut* uecta rati spumosa ad litora Diae
> uenerit, aut *ut* eam deuinctam lumina somno
> liquerit immemori discedens pectore coniunx?

(Poem 64, 116-23)

Once again what Catullus says is possible Latin, though the construction is much commoner in Greek, and the concentrated repetition of *ut* here could hardly fail to sound somewhat exotic. The normal Latin equivalent of the Greek construction is the accusative and infinitive, so that here there is the added advantage of conciseness, because we escape from the heavy prose construction.

Both these Graecisms caught on and are frequent in Augustan poetry. Others, like the use of the nominative and infinitive,

> ait fuisse nauium celerrimus
>
> (Poem 4, 2)

proved less popular.

These details of language, like the new attention to structure and the interpenetration of simple sense with elaborate imagery (as in Poem 7), build up a picture of a movement about which two final generalizations are, perhaps, useful. Firstly, this is hard poetry—not for the general public, but for the lettered *élite* who have the culture needed to appreciate its subtleties and the enthusiasm for tracking them down.[39] Secondly, it is the poetry of art for art's sake, the poetry of *littérature pure*: above all in its most serious productions at the highest level of intent (Poems 63, 64, 66), but also in the *nugae*, the uselessness of which is deliberately emphasized. The antithetical force and the programmatic character of the words in Poem 1

> namque tu solebas
> meas esse aliquid putare nugas.
>
> *For you used to think*
> *these little scraps of verse had real worth.*

are often missed. There is some evidence that in this matter of art for art's sake the *poetae novi* followed a conscious doctrine, provided mainly by Philodemus, the Greek philosopher and poet who lived in Italy and was a contemporary of Catullus. Philodemus was the theorist of a movement to launch a doctrine of the conscious uselessness of poetry.[40]

Both innovations succeeded: Roman poetry remained 'hard', and Roman poets fought to maintain *littérature pure*, despite the efforts of patrons to put poetry again to the service of the community. This is true even of Horace. Despite the occasional high-quality *engagé* political poem and his decision in the last years of his life to support a compromise (the famous *omne tulit punctum qui miscuit utile dulci*),[41] Horace was, in his most creative years as a serious poet, on the whole an adherent of *littérature pure,* just as much as he was, almost everywhere in the *Odes,* an adherent of 'hard' poetry.

On both counts, again, the parallel with our own day is close, and in both contexts we might ask ourselves at what point the heightened possibilities offered to poetry cease to outweigh the consequences of divorce from large sections of the educated public.

CHAPTER V

The Catullan Experience

ANY list of Catullus' best poems is certain to be largely made up of those which were the outcome of the poet's liaison with Lesbia. We do not have to become sentimental about the affair itself (as many have done), or hold it in any historical sense one of the great loves of history, in order to feel that through this affair something happened to make Catullus into a first-rate poet—head and shoulders, as far as we can tell, above the other *poetae novi*. Without this experience to set fire to the talent of its leading poet, the Catullan revolution might well not have found the impetus to transcend the level of sophisticated trifling with dilettante genres that the fragments of his contemporaries and the more certain evidence of a sizeable minority of the poems of Catullus himself suggest as the context in which he began to tackle the writing of serious poetry. Poem 50 is filled with the exhilaration of making verse, but it shows as yet no awareness that verse could provide an outlet for things deeply felt, or stimulate the urge to discover how adequately to express ideas for which words are not easily found. The battle to find the right words for that which the poet dimly but deeply feels, but which resists, or eludes, expression is perhaps the task that tests a poet most. Today we have a long poetic tradition to tell us this. Catullus had practically to make the discovery for himself. When he had made it, there are signs this problem of expression quickly came to fascinate him more than the woman who had made him aware of the problem's existence. As a result he crowded into what hitherto had been regarded as a tenuous literary genre the fullest efforts of his most serious poetic endeavour. This happened not only when he wrote of Lesbia, but in many of the other short poems as well. In the long poems the complex pattern of erudition and ingenuity became infused with a new seriousness of intent. To the poet's function as an artist is added the role of thinker, in so far as he is henceforth concerned with reducing difficult or novel thought to effective and communicable form. This revolution affected the whole future course of poetry. During the next fifty years of Roman poetry its consequences are apparent. The result is not always clear gain, notably with Propertius, who tends to allow his preoccupation with intellectual subtleties to strangle a genuine but ill-developed imaginative spontaneity and to condone an over-slovenly attitude towards freshness of subject-matter.

The Lesbia episode has so stimulated the imagination of literary historians[1] one might well hesitate to scrutinize afresh the details of it, even if they were relevant to an evaluation of Catullus' poetry. How irrelevant instead *Erlebnis* can be to *Dichtung* in this particular context, how unrelated the raw material of poetry to the poetry that genius and inspiration make out of that raw material, has been well expressed in an ironical poem by Mr Auden:

> *The living girl's your business (some odd sorts*
> *Have been an inspiration to men's thoughts):*
> *Yours may be old enough to be your mother,*
> *Or have one leg that's shorter than the other,*
> *Or play Lacrosse or do the Modern Dance,*
> *To you that's destiny, to us it's chance;*
> *We cannot love your love till she take on,*
> *Through you, the wonders of a paragon.*[2]

If Lesbia was Clodia,[3] the affair was, likely enough, a pretty sordid one. Our suspicions find confirmation in Poem 68, where the gulf between the idealized Lesbia and reality is unusually transparent—a result of the mood of dejection (following the death of Catullus' brother) in which the poem was left not fully finished. In Horace's hands, the liaison might have led to the condensed realism of *Odes* III. 20, or IV. 13. With Catullus we get instead a synthesis of reality and fantasy that at first surprises us. We might have expected this sophisticated young man, instead of idealizing the liaison, to deal with it with the slick cynicism we find in the other love poems where Lesbia does not figure (e.g. in Poems 6, 10, 55), or in something closer to the atmosphere of sordid folly with which Lucretius invests passionate love. Consider how accurately Lucretius' words apply, if only the point of view is changed, to the life and the emotions that Catullus made poetry of in the Lesbia poems:

> adde quod absumunt uiris pereuntque labore. . . .
> nequiquam, quoniam medio de fonte leporum
> surgit amari aliquid quod in ipsis floribus angat,
> aut cum conscius ipse animus se forte remordet
> desidiose agere aetatem lustrisque perire.[4]

> *They consume their strength moreover. They are undone*
> *   by their efforts. . . .*
> *To no purpose, since from the source itself of their happi-*
> *   ness*
> *bitter torture surges while their passion still is blooming.*
> *Or a chance pang of remorse and in their minds the thought*
> *how idle, how pointless, is a life that is wasted on lust.*

What should interest us, therefore, about the affair is not the actual circumstances, but how it broke the narrow bounds the new poetry had as yet accepted. To get a feeling for the shape of this transcending experience that is involved, it is convenient to look first at a more self-consciously analytic poet dealing with similar feelings—Propertius. In a well-known elegy of the second book (II. 13. 36), Propertius asks Cynthia when he is dead to have carved on his tombstone the words:

> 'unius hic quondam seruus amoris erat'
> *'He used to be the slave of a single love.'*

There is more here than the protestation, trite to a modern ear, that the lover will be faithful to his mistress 'until death do them part'. Though, of course, that is an obvious assertion

for the passionate lover to make and Propertius makes it often
enough, in just the spirit in which this sort of thing is still
said:

> at me non aetas mutabit tota Sibyllae,
>   non labor Alcidae, non niger ille dies.
> tu mea compones et dices 'Ossa, Properti,
>   haec tua sunt? eheu tu mihi certus eras,
> certus eras eheu, quamuis nec sanguine auito
>   nobilis et quamuis non ita diues eras.' [5]

Age will not change me though I live a Sibyl's years.
Not Hercules' labour, not death's black hour.
That day these will be your words, 'Propertius, ashes now
—or is it really so? You were faithful to me once.
Alas! how faithful, though not of noble line,
or ancient blood, or richer than the next.'

But the phrase *seruus unius amoris,* if it sounds to us like a
cliché we know, was by no means this for Propertius. It had a
kind of programmatic character, labelling what we should
now call a way of life, one that was in some degree excep-
tional, or at any rate sharply opposed to another more tradi-
tional way. Being in love could not constitute a way of life so
long as sexual love was regarded as a regrettable but harm-
less aberration of youth.[6] Love affairs so viewed obviously
lacked seriousness and any kind of substantial, intellectual
satisfaction. Love was not something that gave a new meaning
to life—it simply interfered.[7] Man was an intellectual crea-
ture, as Aristotle had stated, and the proper occupation for
his leisure was philosophy. Roman personal poetry of the
first century B.C., however, challenged this concept. It is put-
ting things only just a little too clearly[8] to say that the elegiac
poets actually thought of their new way of life as opposed to
the traditional 'philosophical' life that seems, rather strangely
to us, to have been the usual outlet for *otium* among the
educated Romans of the first century B.C. We may well
imagine some emancipation of men's minds from the fascina-
tion of moral philosophy was overdue. Few of us today can

share, or even endure, Cicero's voracious appetite for moral philosophy. The new way of life of Catullus and the elegiac poets, though we may doubt the wholesomeness of its continued preoccupation with self and sensuality, must at the outset, if we are frank, cause almost a sigh of relief. The way in which the lover's life is constantly opposed in elegy to the soldier's life is based on the same assumption that for a chosen few (the poets of love) being in love constitutes a way of life, justifiable on more or less serious grounds.

It was usual and traditional to engage in the pursuit of love. But usual and traditional, too, that one's affairs should remain at a casual level and be frequent. The literary tradition is as old in Roman poetry as Plautus and Terence—though how far they follow a convention of the Hellenizing stage that does not reflect actual life in Rome is hard to say. It is a situation that is almost inevitable in a society where marriages were arranged for reasons of family or politics (as they were more and more in the last decades of the Republic) and where a girl in her teens was regularly married to a man much older than herself.[9] One is reminded of the young Don Juans for whom Horace in an early satire discusses whether it is worth while running the risk of conducting your affairs with *matronae*, or wiser to stick to *libertinae*.[10] There can be little doubt this is the situation Catullus often reflects with varying degrees of sympathy (e.g. Poems 6, 10, 32, 35, 41-3, 45, 55; apart from occasional details, very little in the elegiac poems). The beginning of Poem 10 is typical:

> Varus me meus ad suos amores
> uisum duxerat e foro otiosum,
> scortillum, ut mihi tum repente uisum est,
> non sane illepidum neque inuenustum.
> huc ut uenimus, incidere nobis
> sermones uarii.

Varus had taken me on a visit to his latest,
finding me in the forum, with time upon my hands.
An attractive wench, my first impression was,
reasonably educated, and not without a certain charm.

*Well, when we got there we began to talk
on a variety of subjects.*

The increasing possibilities of *otium* in the last century of the Republic doubtless increased the scope for this side of life in Rome.[11]

These attachments were essentially sensual ones, but Catullus' treatment should warn us against allowing the brutally rational approach of Horace in *Satires* I. 2 (or the coarseness of *Epodes* 8 and 12) to place them on the lowest level of sensuality. There need be no doubt that the young men in early Roman comedy are to be thought of as feeling genuine passionate attachment to their *meretrices*, and there is every reason to suppose similar relationships a century and a half later, involving young Roman men and perhaps a wider circle of women now, including not only *meretrices* and *libertinae* of varying social status, but also *matronae*.[12] We must be on our guard against the Victorian commentator who tends to treat as a prostitute every mistress who is not her lover's social equal.

Poem 45 of Catullus shows the relationship perhaps in its most civilized form:

> Acmen Septimius suos amores
> tenens in gremio 'mea' inquit 'Acme,
> ni te perdite amo atque amare porro
> omnes sum assidue paratus annos,
> quantum qui pote plurimum perire,
> solus in Libya Indiaque tosta
> caesio ueniam obuius leoni.'
> hoc ut dixit, Amor sinistra ut ante
> dextra sternuit approbationem.
>
>   at Acme leuiter caput reflectens
> et dulcis pueri ebrios ocellos
> illo purpureo ore suauiata,
> 'sic', inquit 'mea uita Septimille,
> huic uni domino usque seruiamus,
> ut multo mihi maior acriorque

ignis mollibus ardet in medullis.'
hoc ut dixit, Amor sinistra ut ante
dextra sternuit approbationem.
   nunc ab auspicio bono profecti
mutuis animis amant amantur.
unam Septimius misellus Acmen
mauult quam Syrias Britanniasque:
uno in Septimio fidelis Acme
facit delicias libidinesque.
quis ullos homines beatiores
uidit, quis Venerem auspicatiorem?

Holding his sweetheart Acme in his lap,
Septimius said, 'If I do not, my darling,
love you to distraction; if I am reluctant
to love you unswervingly in all the years to come—
and as distractedly moreover as ever human can:
then may I, among the roasting sands of Libya, or of India,
run slap into a lion, green eyes and all.'
When this was said, the god of love, on their left hand now
and not their right, sneezed his approbation.
   Whereat Acme, head arching gently backwards,
with those brightly coloured lips began to kiss
the love-drunk eyes of her darling lover.
'Likewise, Septimius my darling, all life to me,
may we ever this one and only master serve.
For a much greater and far fiercer fire
burns within the marrow of my bones!'
When this was said, the god of love, on their left hand now
and not their right, sneezed his approbation.
   With good omen thus they began their journey into love.
Now each lover's loved with responsive passion:
poor Septimius would rather have his Acme
than the whole of Syria and of Britain;
while Acme, faithful to Septimius alone,
in all love's delights is co-operative.
Who ever saw human beings happier,
or affair embarked on with better omen?

It is obvious from a first reading of these poems how far we are from the atmosphere of the Lesbia poems. These are relationships where talk of 'hopeless love' can only be the rhetorical exaggeration that it is, probably, in Poem 35, 12. Anything even remotely approaching the horror of the *taeter morbus* of Poem 76 is unthinkable, even if we make all possible allowance for differences between comic-satiric treatment and seriously passionate treatment:

> me miserum aspicite et, si uitam puriter egi,
>   eripite hanc pestem perniciemque mihi,
> quae mihi subrepens imos ut torpor in artus
>   expulit ex omni pectore laetitias.
> non iam illud quaero, contra me ut diligat illa,
>   aut, quod non potis est, esse pudica uelit:
> ipse ualere opto et taetrum hunc deponere morbum.
>   o di, reddite mi hoc pro pietate mea.

(Poem 76, 19-26)

There *is* inflation of language here, and a self-righteousness that makes us feel a little uncomfortable. But the reason for it is not insincerity, but rather the opposite: because he takes the situation *so* seriously, the poet draws, as yet, too ingenuously upon the high style of the epic-tragic tradition. (Compare Poem 8, translated page 93, where the situation has the same passionate seriousness, but where the poet has evolved a maturer style for its expression.)

> *Look on me, gods, in my anguish. Have I lived a decent*
>   *life?*
> *Expel then this ruinous pestilence from me.*
> *This languor of disease, stealing into my inmost being,*
> *that has driven all joy from my heart.*
> *I ask no longer that she return the love I bear her;*
> *or that she be faithful to her lover—she is incapable of that.*
> *But give me health, I pray, free me from this disease I*
>   *loathe.*
> *Ye gods, grant me this if I have honoured you.*

Propertius takes some pains to emphasize the difference

between the traditional passionate but transitory infatuation and what had happened to him. His greater explicitness may be used as a kind of commentary on the Lesbia poems. In Propertius II. 25, we have an apology for those who, like himself, are *unius serui amoris*. The point is made from the first word of the elegy:

Vnica nata meo pulcherrima cura dolori
Sole cause of sorrow, unparalleled beauty, my destiny.

Propertius goes on to identify himself with the tradition of Catullus and Calvus (line 4; cf. II. 34. 87-90, where their single loves are named). This, Propertius says, is his 'destiny' (*sors mea,* line 2). A love from which there is no retirement (lines 5-10. Cf. the different attitude of the Don Juan in Horace, *Odes* III. 26). A life of hardships, but one which Propertius is determined to endure (lines 11-20). Lines 21-38 are an apostrophe of the typical imaginary *seruus unius amoris* and an opportunity for a series of *praecepta.* The remainder of the poem contrasts Propertius' attitude with the usual one (lines 39-48), arguing the paradox that, contrary to the arguments usually advanced (by the Don Juans as opposed to the *serui*), there is not greater safety in numbers.[13]

The group addressed (*uos,* line 39) is more than a collection of ninepins assembled for attack. We meet them in the first elegy of Propertius, lines 25-6:

et uos, qui sero lapsum reuocatis, amici,
quaerite non sani pectoris auxilia

Too late, friends, you call back your fallen companion.
Seek help for a mind no longer whole.

The vocative *amici* is the clue. Compare Horace, *Epode* 11. 23-6, where again the lover's *amici* are powerless to help him:

nunc gloriantis quamlibet mulierculam
uincere mollitie amor Lycisci me tenet.
unde expedire non amicorum queant
libera consilia nec contumeliae graues.

It's Lyciscus now I love, who boasts he can outdo
any mere wench in grace and charm.
The advice of friends still free cannot loose me
from his clutches, though they upbraid me roundly.

These passages could be multiplied. They provide a series
of hints about the social background from which Roman per-
sonal poetry emerged. The normal pattern is a group of
amici, a sort of combination (at any rate where poetry and
poets are involved) of the Greek symposium and the Roman
literary circle. Women play, as they did still in Hellenistic
Greece, a secondary role.[14] The men meet at parties, write one
another letters in verse about incidents of sophisticated life,
including their love affairs. These may be, as in comedy, pas-
sionate, but they are primarily on a physical level—though a
scortillum is expected to show some sophistication: see Catul-
lus, Poem 10; cf. Horace, *Odes* II. 11. 21-4. But, as in
Greece, the real bonds of equality, affection and intellectual
sympathy are between men (as when Varus takes Catullus to
meet his latest conquest) and references to homosexuality are
not uncommon.[15] Catullus' disclaimer, so often quoted, in
Poem 16 on the difference between poetry and reality

> nam castum esse decet pium poetam
> ipsum, uersiculos nihil necesse est;
> qui tum denique habent salem ac leporem,
> si sunt molliculi ac parum pudici.

> *The true poet must himself be pure.*
> *His verse is free from such an obligation.*
> *In fact it really can't have wit or charm*
> *unless it's just a little naughty and improper.*

refers, probably, to this sort of poetry and not, as it is almost
ludicrous to suppose, to the Lesbia poem, Poem 5. One feels
these poems of Catullus earlier in time than the Lesbia poems,
but this need not be so: Virgil's second Eclogue shows how
an alternation of interests was possible.

The young men involved in the normal, casual affairs

spent, it seems, their evenings at parties, before making their way through the streets to find, or rejoin, their mistress for the remainder of the night, as we find Propertius doing in I. 3. Or they find their mistress has locked her door and will not open it to them, which provides them with an opportunity to serenade her.[16] From time to time a member of a circle of *amici* becomes the victim of a fresh infatuation. His silence at parties is noticed, and he is subjected to good-natured teasing, as in Horace, *Epode* 11; *Odes* I. 27; Propertius III. 25; etc. At the same time the *amici* are vigilant in case their friend makes too much of a fool of himself: cf. the concern, partly ironic, partly genuine, of Catullus in Poem 55 to find Camerius, who has dropped his *amici* in the excitement of a new affair.

The love poems of Horace are regularly set in this milieu. Horace was not the lukewarm lover some critics would have it he is: he was consciously making poetry out of what was typical of the society of his day. Catullus, too, as Poem 6 and Poem 10 show, could make these affairs the subject-matter of verse. Compare with these Poem 55, lines 15-22:

> dic nobis ubi sis futurus, ede
> audacter, committe, crede luci.
> nunc te lacteolae tenent puellae?
> si linguam clauso tenes in ore,
> fructus proicies amoris omnes.
> uerbosa gaudet Venus loquella.
> uel, si uis, licet obseres palatum,
> dum uestri sim particeps amoris.

Tell us where it is you'll be. Come,
boldly share the secret, give it light of day.
Some fair-skinned beauty holds you? Good!
But if your tongue is held and your mouth is sealed,
you throw away all love's profit.
It's the man who talks and talks brings Venus pleasure.
Though lock your lips in silence if you will,
so long as I am let into the secret.

80

It is wrongheaded to call this sort of poetry superficial or insincere. In it the interest is not in true love, but in the opportunities for urbane ironical observation that the traditional transitory attachments afforded.[17]

But in Catullus and Propertius we find as well a different kind of love. In his poetry, and in some way also in actual experience, Catullus became involved in a kind of love that, in his view of it, transcended the usual pattern, that lifted him out of the circle of *amici* into a more deeply passionate relationship with a woman who, because he wanted her as his intellectual companion as well, gave shape to a new conception of a kind of *amor* that could also be *amicitia*.[18]

This does not necessarily mean that Catullus' affair was unique in reality. Poem 68 shows how prone Catullus was to idealization and to self-deception. The actual affair was only the starting point necessary to give Catullus the initial concept of a new and exciting ideal love. If that concept had been more fully realized by the actual affair, he might have been less impelled to create the illusion of it in his poetry. The actual affair could well have remained on the level of the liaison between Varus and his *scortillum* in Poem 10, though generating more sparks—and perhaps, in Clodia's view, it did remain there. It is Catullus' vision of the attachment which created the *docta puella* that dominated Roman love poetry henceforth.

Catullus soon discovered that this new kind of love, despite the hope it gave of lasting *amicitia*, could end, like the usual type of affair, in 'betrayal'. By the time this stage is reached, he is almost certainly less concerned with the real Lesbia than with solving the linguistic and poetic problems he faced in expressing the conflict in himself between the residue of physical attachment and intellectual awareness of its folly.[19]

By the time we get to Propertius, Catullus' discovery that intenser love brings intenser pain has become common knowledge. Propertius, in his role of poet who is *seruus unius amoris*, is less concerned with the horror of 'betrayal' than with exploring the variety of emotions aroused by a love that

G

was intenser for the man than the usual kind. So intense it tore the poet from his friends, gave the hope of lasting longer —he would even pretend to hope it would last for life. With the traditional attachments it would have been ridiculous to pretend that they could hope to survive into old age, when passion is either dead or ugly. In compensation, this kind of love makes demands upon the man that cause him to feel more like a slave than a free man.[20] This is the origin of the *seruitium amoris* cliché and the consequent use of *domina* for the mistress, concepts not found prior to Roman personal poetry.[21] The reason is quite simply that, prior to Catullus, this kind of attachment, or rather this kind of attitude to a mistress, did not exist. The free man differs from the slave, we say today, in that he can change his job. The *liber amans*, if the course of free love did not run smooth, was not tied to one mistress. But the new type of lover, like the slave, though he tried to run away, could not. He even actually accepts his unhappy state, so permanent is his fidelity to his *domina*. Moreover, the new type of mistress is more often of the social status to be reasonably thought of as having actual slaves in real life, so that the plea 'let me be one of your slaves' is reasonable. Addressed to a common prostitute, it could hardly fail to sound ridiculous. Once the *seruitium amoris* cliché is launched, of course every poet has his *domina*, and even Horace and those who cling to the older pattern can toy with the new cliché.

Reconstructions of the social background may seem a precarious basis for critical judgments, especially of a poet so remote from us and so little known as Catullus. Yet the Catullan revolution is in more ways than one a social phenomenon, as we saw earlier, and we cannot avoid occasional recourse to probing the reality that produced the poetry. We must remember, however, our primary concern is poetry, not social history. It is sufficient for our purpose to recognize the effects of the poet's perceiving in the relationship of man with woman fresh complexities of exhilaration and despair.

As a source of poetry, the Lesbia affair is more significant than the other great emotional experience in Catullus' life of which we know—the death of his brother. There is no certain sign in Catullus' poetry of his brother's death, apart from the references to it in Poem 65, beyond one splendid poem (101) and one rather unsatisfactory one (68), and only of Poem 101 can it be said that the *chose vécue* has poetry made out of it. The melancholy that pervades 68 and which produced that curious poem could be the result of any experience affecting the poet deeply, and was in fact not an experience of an unusual kind. And in any case, there is more of Lesbia in Poem 68 than there is of the brother. Some recent critics have made much of the brother's death;[22] but, except in the negative sense that it may have stopped him temporarily from writing poetry, it is difficult to see more than a limited significance in it for his poetry.

The Lesbia affair was beyond doubt very different. The *chose vécue* had poem after poem made directly out of it, in deep contrast to the traditional superficiality of the other love poems—written earlier in time perhaps, or simply at a different level of intent at moments when the poet was free of commanding emotion. Moreover, the longer poems also show that the poet is drawing upon this experience for a more subtle analysis of passion (not so grand as the divine madness of Greek tragedy, but more real and less negative), in order to make poetry out of material that is formally distinct from himself. The Lesbia affair, having made a different person of Catullus, made different persons of Ariadne and of Attis as well. Finally, the experience, or rather the violence and direction of the poet's reaction to it, seems highly unusual in ancient society and not to have been drawn upon for the making of poetry before, though it set a fashion. It is clear that Propertius and Tibullus, among other successors of Catullus, considered they were writing about the same kind of experience. If, somehow, they cannot bring it off as well in their poetry, we should not try to explain the uniqueness of Catullus in terms of uniqueness of experience: his type of affair probably became more and more common in the last century of the

Republic. The relative failure of Augustan elegists lies in the fact that they became obsessed with trying to make poetry out of an identical experience. The tragedy of Roman personal poetry is that a subtle technique for the linguistic exploration of the poet's inward conflict was inherited by poets whose inward life, apart from their enthusiasm for love and poetry, contained little that urgently needed expression.

CHAPTER VI

The Beginnings of Modern Lyric

MANY of the changes to which the New Poetry gave poetic expression were doubtless in the air. The increasing sophistication of Roman society, the product of growing material ease and national consciousness, brought with it an increasing willingness, at any rate on the part of an *élite*, to take poets seriously as people. The same tendency led to an impatience with outworn poetic conventions now outmoded by the rapid development of a complex and characteristic Latin prose style, and a day-to-day acquaintance with the problems of expression. The earliest speeches of Cicero precede the Catullan movement by about a decade, the earliest extant letters date from the years of its beginnings.

Roman culture was reaching a stage of development where it could compete with Greek on a new basis. The New Poetry was not, however, the abrupt recourse to alien importation, an attempt to transplant exotic tastes, that some assume. The amount of direct, unassimilated borrowing from Greek literature was a good deal less than took place, for example, at the time of the first great wave of Roman poetry in the second half of the third century B.C. In style, structure and, to a limited degree, subject-matter also, the New Poetry was firmly rooted in Roman traditions. The sudden swerve the new movement imparted to the subsequent course of Roman literature is due more to the unique stature of a single very individual poet than to a sudden influx of foreign fashion.

It happens we have seen in the present century a change in the course of English poetry as abrupt, superficially, as that brought about by the Catullan revolution. There are similarities between the two movements, and I have tried to avail myself of them. They offer a valid tool for criticism to use—provided we remember constantly the two movements are remote in time, largely unrelated, and, of course, far from identical.

Writing poetry is like engaging in love or in politics. In whatever age and society you live, a number of the fundamental problems of constructing a poem, of understanding the experience of love, or of governing a country are alike. The student of anthropology and the student of political science know this. They move freely from age to age and culture to culture, trying to isolate the basic problems and man's attempts to deal with them. The literary historian, over-impressed by differences of language, tends to study the poetry of one language too exclusively, not realizing how general are the problems that the poet has to struggle with in organizing his material into a poem, and how readily similar solutions can arise independently of direct commerce across linguistic frontiers.

This kind of comparative literature needs, however, an historical context, or else we miss real differences and the emergence of genuine innovations. It cannot be wholly irrelevant to an evaluation for the critic to realize that something is happening in literature for the first time. One major purpose of this book has been to sketch the ways in which the New Poetry took shape. It will be useful, perhaps, to conclude with some reflections on important ways in which it does or does not measure up to our preconception of what short personal poems should be. For, while some of the poetry of Catullus is good enough to arouse the kind of appreciation that is directed by simple emotional appeal, a good deal more of it requires a more informed view, and our appreciation of the best can hardly be impaired by a keener perception of the poet's intentions or a juster appraisal of the formal resources the poet could command. Let us consider first one important new feature which by itself made the New Poetry more like our modern lyric poetry, and then some related features where we can see only the beginnings in Catullus of that type of short, lyric poem which today is so common that we tend to regard it as the normal manifestation of the impulse to make poetry.

THE POET'S AUDIENCE

The way in which the sophisticated young men we meet in Catullus took themselves and their writing seriously inevitably encouraged in their verse an independence of their audience quite out of the pattern of the relationship of the artist to ancient society. The personal genius of Catullus and the special circumstances that sharpened his inspiration forced his readers to accept a new relationship between audience and poet. It has become usual since, and that fact masks for us how unusual it must have been when Catullus began writing. Some of the early Greek lyric poets were exceptions perhaps to the general rule. Their poetry is now so fragmentary, however, that critical discussion of it is exposed to the constant risk of reading into bits of poems qualities that poetry only later took on when the evolution of personal poetry began afresh in Rome.

In general, the work of art in antiquity was an act of service to the community and one that sought consciously the community's approval. The *poetae novi* thrust the educated community at large aside from this traditional position at the centre of the poet's intentions while writing. Less concerned with his public audience, the poet became concerned first with an intimate clique, and ultimately with himself.

The first consequence of this is a measure of unintelligibility to the outsider, because the poet does not bother to inform him fully about what is going on. This disturbs no reader familiar with contemporary poetry, but it has in the past puzzled and exasperated scholars grown accustomed to the public character that ancient literature elsewhere possesses, and the degree to which, normally, the ancient writer reveals secrets of circumstance and allusion to painstaking research. Kroll puts the essence of the matter very simply:

eben weil Catull oft aus der Situation heraus für sich und nicht für den Leser dichtete, bleibt die Veranlassung des einzelnen Liedes oft ganz im Dunkeln.[1]

Kroll's remark, quite clearly, carries overtones of reproach.

Audiences, however, are of different kinds and the relationship between an audience and the participants in the spectacle being watched will vary. To take fairly extreme examples: the audience at a successful modern comedy and the audience watching an operation being performed by a distinguished surgeon will have obviously dissimilar reactions. The difference of significance to us here between the two spectacles is that the second involves things that do not take place, *primarily*, because the audience is there, or for its benefit. A lot of poetry from Catullus onwards is rather like the surgical operation, in that it does not come into being, *primarily*, for the sake of its ultimate audience. Though, of course, once the process of making the poem is complete, if it is a good poem it has significance for selected outsiders. The change is in emphasis, it is not a complete transformation: Catullus continues to keep his eventual audience at the back of his mind, as occasional hints show.[2] But it is a shift of enormous importance for the character of the poem produced. Like a good surgeon, too, Catullus interpolates here and there a certain amount of explanatory comment to let his audience know enough for Catullus' purpose of what is going on. (This becomes occasionally obvious—when, for example, the addressee is told things he obviously knows already.[3])

It is likely this new relationship of poet to audience was created by the *poetae novi* almost accidentally. The impulse to create preceded thoughts of publication. But once the audience came to accept this way of writing poetry—being reduced to overhearing the performance, as it were, instead of commanding it—the progress the changed relationship permitted is obvious. When poetry is written on the reduced scale that the New Poetry exploited, the gains are particularly important. Here, provided the poet gave the uninitiated reader—or hearer—outside the poet's small original circle, who naturally caught more, just enough to go on, so that he could reconstruct for himself what the limited framework of a short poem prevented setting out in detail, then the economy and the intensity of the new technique are inestimable. It may exasperate our curiosity not to know the exact circumstances in which Asinius stole the table-napkin in Poem 12, but it would weaken the poem if the poet attempted to give us all the facts. Poems of this kind depend for their strength on elliptical treatment of the story. Like a good funny story a poem of this kind depends on a measure of imaginative collaboration from the audience. Tell the audience too much and the story, or the poem, collapses under its own weight. The more subtly organized the poem, the more this is so. When we move to higher levels of intent, it becomes perfectly superfluous for us to be told who the man of Colonia was, for example, in Poem 17, or who the speaker is and whose the˙yacht in Poem 4:

> Phaselus ille, quem uidetis, hospites,
> ait fuisse nauium celerrimus,
> neque ullius natantis impetum trabis
> nequisse praeterire, siue palmulis
> opus foret uolare siue linteo.
> et hoc negat minacis Hadriatici
> negare litus insulasue Cycladas
> Rhodumque nobilem horridamque Thraciam
> Propontida trucemue Ponticum sinum,
> ubi iste post phaselus antea fuit
> comata silua; nam Cytorio in iugo
> loquente saepe sibilum edidit coma.
> Amastri Pontica et Cytore buxifer,
> tibi haec fuisse et esse cognitissima
> ait phaselus: ultima ex origine
> tuo stetisse dicit in cacumine,
> tuo imbuisse palmulas in aequore,
> et inde tot per impotentia freta
> erum tulisse, laeua siue dextera
> uocaret aura, siue utrumque Iuppiter
> simul secundus incidisset in pedem;
> neque ulla uota litoralibus deis
> sibi esse facta, cum ueniret a mari

nouissimo hunc ad usque limpidum lacum.
sed haec prius fuere: nunc recondita
senet quiete seque dedicat tibi,
gemelle Castor et gemelle Castoris.

The yacht you see, gentlemen, over there
was once, she claims, the fastest craft that ever sailed.
There wasn't a vessel afloat, she says, whose speed
she couldn't better, both in a rowing race
and when the conditions stipulated sail.
The surly Adriatic coast, according to her, has got
to admit it. The Cyclades, too,
noble Rhodes, the unkempt Thracian
Propontis and the cruel Pontic gulf.
Where this yacht (as she afterwards became) in former
    time
was leafy forest, and high on Mount Cytorus
her loquacious leaves were often heard to whisper.

Pontic Amastris and Cytorus, rich in boxwood,
this yacht claims your familiarity with these facts.
That—to probe her origins to the source—
she stood, she says, upon your heights,
and dipped her oars in your waters first.
And then, through ocean after raging ocean,
she bore her master, tacking to port and starboard
as the breezes called for—except, that is, when Jove
blew steady on the sails from dead astern.
Not a single vow to landlubber gods was made,
she said, by her in journeying from the ocean's
very edge all the way to this limpid lake.
But all this was long ago. In quiet now,
and in retirement, she dedicates herself to you,
twin Castor, and to you, Castor's twin.

MEDITATIVE LYRIC

Poem 4 is a poem that obviously is of a quality that demands
its being taken seriously as a piece of writing. No modern poet

need be ashamed of the adroitness with which an inherently sentimental situation is handled without sentimentality, while giving full scope to the reminiscent garrulity which the situation requires. Nor is this the only poem which stands on its own feet in this way—or even the best of those that do.

The modern reader of Catullus, however, who reads not poems in isolation but the whole collection, and then glances back to our contemporary poetry in order to attempt some rough overall comparison, will soon feel that in Catullus something modern poetry generally supplies is absent or, at any rate, insufficiently present. This is the introspective note, the meditative character of much modern verse, the impression we are given that, in the course of the poem itself, the poet is marshalling his thoughts and reflections, with the result that these, given poetic structure, become the poem. The path to this kind of writing seems fairly obvious to us, once the poet has freed himself from his subservience to an audience, yet it is not apparent that Catullus advanced far along this path. The result is something quite different from didactic verse, where the poet argues a case with his reader. In this kind of lyric verse (using the term 'lyric' in the modern sense of course), the argument is more often conducted by the poet with himself.

T. S. Eliot once tried to define this type of writing by distinguishing between what he calls the voice of the poet addressing an audience, whether large or small (epic poetry, perhaps), the voice of the poet creating a dramatic character speaking in verse, and the voice of the poet talking to himself —or to nobody. He argues that much modern lyric poetry is of the last kind. Drawing upon a suggestion of a modern German poet, Gottfried Benn, Eliot describes this sort of poem as the product of a creative impulse and the effort of expression itself:

In a poem which is neither didactic nor narrative, and not animated by any other social purpose, the poet may be concerned solely with expressing in verse—using all his resources of words, with their history, their connotations, their music—this obscure impulse. He does not know what he has to say until he has said it; and in the effort to say it he is not concerned with making other people understand anything. He is not concerned, at this stage, with other people at all: only with finding the right words or, anyhow, the least wrong words. He is not concerned whether anybody else will ever listen to them or not, or whether anybody else will ever understand them if he does. He is oppressed by a burden which he must bring to birth in order to obtain relief.[4]

On this point we find Mr Robert Graves in agreement with Eliot:

Poems should not be written, like novels, to entertain or instruct the public; or the less poems they. The pathology of poetic composition is no secret. A poet finds himself caught in some baffling emotional problem, which is of such urgency that it sends him into a sort of trance. And in this trance his mind works, with astonishing boldness and precision, on several imaginative levels at once. The poem is either a practical answer to his problem, or else it is a clear statement of it; and a problem clearly stated is half-way to solution. Some poets are more plagued than others with emotional problems, and more conscientious in working out the poems which arise from them—that is to say more attentive in their service to the Muse.[5]

Let us ask ourselves how far these statements of two major modern poets are helpful as a commentary on Poem 8:

Miser Catulle, desinas ineptire,
et quod uides perisse perditum ducas.
fulsere quondam candidi tibi soles,
cum uentitabas quo puella ducebat
amata nobis quantum amabitur nulla.   5
ibi illa multa cum iocosa fiebant,
quae tu uolebas nec puella nolebat,
fulsere uere candidi tibi soles.
nunc iam illa non uolt: tu quoque inpotens noli,
nec quae fugit sectare, nec miser uiue,   10
sed obstinata mente perfer, obdura.
uale, puella. iam Catullus obdurat,
nec te requiret nec rogabit inuitam.

92

at tu dolebis, cum rogaberis nulla.
scelesta, uae te, quae tibi manet uita?   15
quis nunc te adibit? cui uideberis bella?
quem nunc amabis? cuius esse diceris?
quem basiabis? cui labella mordebis?
at tu, Catulle, destinatus obdura.

Don't be a fool, my poor Catullus. You must stop it
and count as lost what you see is lost.
There was a time when the bright sun shone for you.
She was the leader then and you the ready companion,
and you loved her as none will be loved.
Then there were done those many merry things.
The things you wanted, though she was ready enough.
There is no doubt the bright sun shone for you.
But now it's No she says. Don't be impatient then for Yes.
Do not chase a girl that runs away. Do not live dejected,
but with hardened heart endure it. You must be firm.
Good-bye, woman. Catullus now is firm.
He'll not run to ask a girl that is unwilling.
You'll be sorry when no man wants you.
Worthless woman, what life is left for you?
Who now will come to you? Who think you pretty?
Whom will you love? Whose will they say you are?
Whom will you kiss? Whose lips bite?
Stop Catullus. You must be resolved. You must be firm.

It would be hard to deny that the genesis of a poem like
this is in an impulse of the kind Eliot and Graves describe.
Both, however, being concerned with the genesis of the poem,
rather than the poem itself, pass over an important point,
that such poetry is not static: it is not the outcome of a process
of thought, but a record of the process itself. In Poem 8 the
poet's ideas are not assembled first and then versified. They
unwind as the poem is written. The poem acquires, as it were,
another dimension, as opposed to the flatness (in this sense)
of the generality of ancient poetry. The situation out of which
the poem arises is that moment in a liaison when it becomes

obvious that love has ceased to be mutual. The poet's intellectual perception that this is so cannot restrain a residual attraction to the woman which pulls against the counsels of common sense. Poem 8 starts on a note of resignation with the intellect in control (lines 1-2). This passes to regret at the falling to pieces of what has been a passionate affair (lines 3-5); the poet's thoughts then dwell a moment (lines 6-8) on past happiness, and the image of bright sunshine is repeated more emphatically (*uere* added) in reaffirmation of that happiness. Common sense then reclaims the upper hand (lines 9-11). The poet tries to strengthen his shaky resolution by voicing a formal renunciation (lines 12-13), endeavouring to convince himself it will hurt her as it hurts him (*at tu dolebis*) to be deserted (lines 14 ff.). But gradually, as the series of illustrations of her future privations becomes more detailed and vivid, abuse melts into unconscious evocation of the poet's past happiness, until in sudden realization of what is happening common sense endeavours again in the last line to assert itself.

It is essential if one is to understand Poem 8 to realize the shifting viewpoint and inconsistency of the speaker. To trace, however, the pattern of the sequence of thought is not to exhaust the poem. The tendency of classical literary criticism is to put the emphasis of analysis on the subject-matter of a poem and to underemphasize the complexity, stressed by both Eliot and Graves, of the process of making a poem. As though old Cato were right for all forms of literature when he said 'Rem tene: uerba sequentur'. Eliot's words suggest a very different approach by inviting us to look at Poem 8 as the product of an 'obscure impulse' to expression, a process of 'finding the right words or, anyhow, the least wrong words', instead of dismissing this aspect of the poem as Kroll does when he says: 'Der Aufbau des Gedichtes, das einfache und kaum irgendwo "poetische" Mittel verwendet, ergibt sich folgerichtig aus der Stimmung des Augenblickes.'[6] Instead of judging the qualities of the poem by assessing the emotions that produced it ('diese unbedingte Aufrichtigkeit und Natürlichkeit des Pathos ist tief ergreifend'), should we not try to take account of the complexities of the work of art itself?

It is perhaps even more profitable to look at Poem 76 in this way. Poems 31 and 46 seem likewise to me to derive their quality as poetry more from their status as meditations in a scene, materializations of emotion, as it were, than as descriptions of the scene. But sustained poetry that is clearly of this kind is rare in Catullus, though there are a number of elegiac fragments which battle with the expression of a single complicated idea. For example, Poem 109, which hammers at the need for sincerity and permanence as constituents of true affection. There is enough all the same to point to the emergence of genuine meditative lyric, in contrast to that sort of ancient poetry which lyricizes a static situation or follows a logical, predetermined, evident sequence of thought. This vacillating structure produces good poetry, of course, only as long as the battle to find the least wrong words is real. In this respect Horace seems to me the best Roman personal poet after Catullus: the struggle to turn thought into right words is conducted by Horace with elegance and aplomb, but one can feel the fight is on. But the Romans understood so well the rhetorical counterfeiting of states of mind such as vacillation that the poets were exposed to an unusually strong temptation to remain content with the effect in the absence of adequate antecedent cause. The argumentation of elegy occasionally becomes, therefore, mere textbook mannerism, especially in Ovid.

FORMAL SURVIVALS: THE ADDRESSEE

When, then, we say that much of what was new in the New Poetry resembles, and can be illuminated by, contemporary poetry, what we have in mind is that it is the outcome: firstly, of a comparable view of the poet's function in society (as a creative artist who works undominated by thoughts of his eventual public); secondly, of a comparable endeavour on the part of the poet to record the actual process of his thought (instead of remaining content with what can be clearly, or authoritatively, stated—or simply noting down the out-pourings of his sensibility); and, finally, as we saw in an earlier chapter, of an enthusiasm for exploiting the resources of poetic technique.

The finished product is still fairly different. The thought is more limited in range and displays often a (comparative) ingenuousness that has been mistaken for spontaneity. But it is perhaps the overall *form* of a Catullan poem which is its most fundamentally archaic and remote feature. For the details of structure Catullus was able to draw upon, and transform, a rich poetic tradition. For the problem of how to lay out the whole he had not the same guidance. The short poem, as we understand it today, hardly existed. Its formal layout could not be conjured out of the empty air. What Catullus does, therefore, is to take existing forms and crowd into them a new wealth of content.

The critics have made much here of one comparatively alien form chosen by Catullus for adaptation to his purpose: the Hellenistic Greek epigram. They fail usually to notice how deeply bedded his poetry is as well in traditional native forms, such as the dirge (*neniae*) and the lampoon, or the letter between friends which the Romans were just coming to regard as a form of literature. Even where this formal continuity within the structure of Roman life is recognized, its purpose has not always been understood. To call Poem 3 a parody of a dirge[7] is misleading: rather it is an attempt to make complex, sophisticated poetry out of a traditional unsophisticated verse form.

All these forms have two common characteristics which we no longer find quite natural in poetry. They presuppose a particular set of circumstances for which the poem is written, and they require a particular person to be addressed. It is interesting to consider the degree to which these characteristics stood in the way of the development of meditative lyric.

The short poems of Catullus are mostly either formally addressed to somebody, or at any rate (the very short poems particularly) imply an addressee, and this continued to be usual in Horace and frequent in elegy. Only four of the polymetric poems dispense with an addressee. The omission is much commoner in the elegiac pieces—mainly short epigrams, or Lesbia poems using the short epigram form on a higher level. Questions are common, to give the illusion of an interlocutor. It is obvious how the necessity of appearing to talk to a friend (or an enemy) inhibits the making of a poem into the record purely of a process of thinking. The densely imaginative style of serious poetry, to begin with, is incompatible with any realistically conversational tone. Yet, whether the Roman poet felt self-conscious about writing a poem which had no apparent motivation (such as talking to a friend provides), or whether it is simply that the formal inclusion of an addressee was so regular a convention of the inherited forms which the Roman poets took over that it seemed impossible to suppress it, it is clear the Roman personal poets found it hard to rid themselves of the addressee.

The addressee is not a fundamental feature of modern meditative lyric, and Eliot is not very disturbed by his occasional presence:

I do not deny that a poem may be addressed to one person. . . . But my opinion is, that a good love poem, though it may be addressed to one person, is always meant to be overheard by other people. Surely, the proper language of love—that is, of communication to the beloved and to no one else—is prose.[8]

I am less sure that in ancient poetry we are entitled to look in the same way at poems like Poem 8 (which are essentially meditative) and at poems which (by being formally addressed to another) necessarily take some cognizance of an audience. It is very hard in many of the poems of Catullus to determine to what extent the poem is meant to be 'overheard by other people'.

We may note that the poems I have cited as instances of meditative lyric appear to illustrate two devices for disposing of the addressee. Or perhaps this is putting the evolution at too conscious a level. It might be better to say of these

poems that their different form permitted a freer develop-
ment. In Poems 8, 46 and 76 the addressee is Catullus him-
self.[9] We do not have to be over-subtle and talk of the poet's
awareness of a dichotomy within himself. A poem addressed
to oneself was reconcilable with tradition. Catullus therefore,
while preserving the formal feature, invested it with a new
purpose. In Poems 31 and 44 we have a place addressed—
a device which virtually reduces the poem, formally, to a
monologue, making it readily convertible into a record of a
process of thinking. We may compare the device in Poem 2
of addressing Lesbia's sparrow:

> Passer, deliciae meae puellae,
> quicum ludere, quem in sinu tenere,
> cui primum digitum dare appetenti
> et acris solet incitare morsus,
> cum desiderio meo nitenti
> carum nescio quid lubet iocari,
> et solaciolum sui doloris,
> credo, ut tum grauis acquiescat ardor:
> tecum ludere sicut ipsa possem
> et tristis animi leuare curas!

Sparrow, source of pleasure to her I love,
with you she often plays and holds you to her breast,
offering fingertip to eager beak,
soliciting your darting nip.
(For there are moments when my radiant love
finds a kind of comfort in this idle play.
You are a consolation in her pain. She hopes
to soothe, I feel, her brooding love thereby.)
I wish I could, like her, play and sport with you,
and lighten trouble's burden in my heart.[10]

Tradition is strong enough still to permit addressing the
sparrow, though to us it would be much more natural to
begin with a simple statement, or perhaps a short piece of
narrative ('When I saw Lesbia yesterday with her sparrow
. . . I thought'). It may be suspected the tradition of the

addressee came to creak a little even in Roman poetry. Horace, of course, continues the trick of the non-personal addressee in the *Odes* (e.g. III. 13). More often he reduces the addressee to the status of recipient of the finished poem (perhaps like Catullus, Poems 56 and 113), rather in the way that some modern poets put at the head of a poem that it is 'for' so-and-so.[11] Propertius uses this external addressee, too, and he is the first Roman poet to dispense at all regularly with an addressee entirely.[12] Catullus, however, is only on the threshold of the exploitation of these devices and their final abandonment, though we may ask ourselves how many of the Lesbia poems containing her name in the vocative are in any real sense verse epistles (as they have, so to speak, to pretend to be) and not in reality meditative lyrics in the modern sense.

We have to remember how maddeningly scrappy after all Catullus' little book is, especially when we start to strip off the poems written at the lower levels of intent. Among those that are left there are many about whose whole tone and intention we must remain unsure. To understand these at all, it is essential to regard Catullus not as an isolated phenomenon, but as a forerunner of a new kind of poetry, the truly fruitful development of which continued for fifty years after his death.[13] We must study these scraps of poetry alert for traces of themes and attitudes which we find fully developed in the poetry of the Augustan age. Only in this way can we arm ourselves against their provocative elusiveness. At the same time we realize how close the connections are between Catullus and the poets of the next generation, and how considerable Catullus' contribution was to what they achieved. This kind of interpretation is less precarious than it sounds. Its product, rightly handled, is not strained conjecture, but an occasional sudden flash of understanding which from time to time illuminates what had seemed too incomplete to grant us any sense of poetic quality, or even meaning.

There was not a continuous rise in quality. The half-century of Roman personal poetry that followed Catullus produced several outstanding poets and a certain amount of first-rate original poetry. The movement, however, was dominated by the Catullan revolution to an extent that quickly proved pernicious. The elegiac poets seem to us to be following too slavishly, to be attempting to make poetry out of the repeated recapture of an experience whose artistic freshness could scarcely be recreated. The tyranny that the Catullan revolution imposed, as a result of the dominating prestige of its chief revolutionary, is shown by the curious phenomenon of Propertius: a poet clearly of exceptional and original talent who seems simply unable to find subjects adequate and congenial to his powers. Only Horace perhaps found, in the poetry of reflection instead of the poetry of passionate utterance, a recipe for reconciling individuality with communicable experience.

Notes

CHAPTER I

1. For a good outline of trends in criticism and what he calls their 'protest against the obscuring of literary values by a cloud of facts', see W. H. Bruford, *Literary Interpretation in Germany*, Cambridge inaugural lecture, 1952. The influence nineteenth-century German *Philologie* exercises still on literary criticism need hardly be pointed out. For sensible comment in this connection related to a single poem (Poem 35) of Catullus, see F. O. Copley, *A.J.Ph.*, 1953, 149-60. E. Fraenkel's insistence in his *Horace* (1957) that all the data we need for understanding a poem are contained in it is very relevant to Catullan studies.

2. T. S. Eliot, 'Dante', in *Selected Essays* (1932), p. 237.

3. See R. G. C. Levens, 'Catullus', in *Fifty Years of Classical Scholarship*, ed. M. Platnauer (1955).

4. For a full and perceptive review, see A. Rostagni, *Letteratura latina* (2nd ed., 1954), vol. i.

5. A. L. Wheeler, *Catullus and the Traditions of Ancient Poetry*, Sather Classical Lectures, 1928 (1934).

6. A. Guillemin, 'L'élément humain dans l'élégie latine', *R.E.L.*, 1940, 95.

7. By E. A. Barber in his useful review of Hellenistic poetry in *Fifty Years of Classical Scholarship*, ed. M. Platnauer (1955).

8. We really know nothing about the life of Catullus. A few poems can be linked with known dates and the dates of other poems inferred from these. The identification of Lesbia with Clodia, sister of P. Clodius Pulcher (died 52 B.C.) and wife of Q. Metellus Celer (died before March 59 B.C.) seems certain. For the knowable facts and full references, see H. J. Mette, *Gnomon*, 1956, 34-8. The datable poems are:

Poem 35: Not earlier than 59 B.C. (the name Nouum Comum dates from 59).

Poem 83: Not later than 59 B.C. (if the *uir* is Metellus).

Poem 51: Not later than 59 B.C. (if the *ille* is Metellus).

Poems 46 and 101: Probably written while Catullus was attached to the *cohors* of Memmius (probably pro-praetor of Bithynia-Pontus 57-56 B.C.).

Poem 68: Probably written before Catullus' departure for Bithynia. Perhaps Poems 65-6 also.

Poems 4; 9; 10; 12; 28; 31; 47: Probably written after Catullus' return from Bithynia.

Poem 113: Refers to the second consulship of Pompey (55 B.C.) as a recent event.

Poem 53: Refers to the speech of Calvus against Vatinius (probably 55 B.C.).

Poem 55: Refers to the *ambulatio* of the theatre of Pompey (consecrated 55 B.C.).

Poem 11: Refers to Caesar's expedition to Britain (first expedition, autumn 55 B.C.).

Here are dates of a kind for a score of poems. Round this framework of a writing life, beginning some time before 59 B.C. and extending some time beyond 55 B.C., some conjectural grouping of other poems (e.g. the Lesbia and the Vatinius poems) seems possible. We have, then, a reasonably probable *floruit*, but little of value either biographically or critically. For the chronology of the Lesbia poems, Mette resorts to a tissue of inferences hardly as conducive to certainty as sensible guesswork based on the internal evidence of the Lesbia poems themselves. The only other ancient source, Jerome, is clearly faulty and almost valueless. [See A. Rostagni, *Svetonio De poetis* (1944), p. 60.]

9. *Satires* I. 4. 62.

10. *Annals* 181-85W.

11. *Annals* 186-93W.

12. The fact that, according to Gellius (XII. 4. 4-5), Ennius slipped himself into Book VII of the *Annals* disguised as an historical character shows how completely disassociated poet and work of art were. See Fr. Klingner, *Dichter und Dichtkunst im alten Rom* (1947) [reprinted in *Römische Geisteswelt* (1956)].

13. hoc erat, experto frustra Varrone Atacino
atque quibusdam aliis, melius quod scribere possem.

(*Satires* I. 10. 46-7.)

14. *Satires* I. 4. 45-62.

15. Ibid., 41-4.

16. *Satires* I. 10. 7-14.

17. The texts are, of course, in Morel, *F.P.L.*, but may otherwise not be readily available. For a translation of the relevant passage of Gellius and for full comment, see Wheeler, op. cit., pp. 61-86. For a briefer, but more perceptive assessment, see A. Rostagni, *Letteratura latina* (2nd ed., 1954), i, pp. 311-16. The question whether there was a school around L. Catulus is dealt with in H. Bardon, *La littérature latine inconnue*, i (1952), p. 124.

18. The fragments are given in alphabetical order of first lines. For good comment on Laevius, see Bardon, op. cit., pp. 189-95.

aut
nunc quaepiam alia te puella
Asiatico ornatu affluens
aut Sardiano aut Lydio
fulgens decore et gratia
pellicuit?

complexa somno corpora
operiuntur ac suaui quie
dicantur.

corpore pectoreque undique obeso ac
mente exsensa, tardigemulo
senio oppressum . . .

cupidius miserulo obito

delphino cinctis uehiculis hippocampisque asperis

etsi ne utiquam, quid foret expauida grauis
dura fera asperaque famultas, potui dominio
accipere superbo . . .

fac papyrina haec terga habeant stigmata

gracilenticolorem
dum ex hoc gracilans fit.

hac qua sol uagus igneas habenas
inmittit propius iugatque terrae.

humum umidum pedibus fodit.

lasciuiterque ludunt

lex Licinia introducitur
lux liquidula haedo redditur.

mea Vatiena amabo

meminens Varro corde uolutat

nocte dieque
decretum et auctum

nocte ut opertus amictu
latibulet uir

num quod meum admissum nocens
hostit uoluntatem tuam?

nunc Laertie belle para
ire Ithacam.

omnes sunt denis syllabis uersi

philtra omnia undique eruunt:
antipathes illud quaeritur,
trochiscili, ungues, taeniae,
radiculae, herbae, surculi,
saurae, illices bicodulae,
hinnientium dulcedines.

scabra in legendo reduuiosaue offendens

sed iam purporeo suras include cothurno
et reuocet uolucres in pectore balteu sinus,
pressaque iam grauida crepitent tibi terga pharetra;
derige odorisequos ad caeca cubilia canes.

seque in alta maria praecipem misit
inops aegra sanitatis herois

subductisupercilicarptores

tunc irruunt, cachinnos
ioca dicta risitantes.

tu qui permensus ponti maria alta
ueliuola

ubi ego saepe petris

Venerem igitur almum adorans,
siue femina siue mas est,
ita ut alma Noctiluca est . . .

Venus amoris altrix,
genetrix cupiditatis,
mihi quae diem serenum
hilarula praepandere cresti,
opseculae tuae ac ministrae . . .

19. Compare Ennius, *Medea*, 253-61W, with the opening lines of
Catullus, Poem 64.

20. To take one detail of vocabulary that has been systematically
studied: when Catullus wishes to describe a ship on the sea he turns to
Ennius. See the comparative tables of words and expressions in E. de Saint
Denis, *Le rôle de la mer dans la poésie latine* (1935).

21. The best review of Greek influences is contained in D. Braga,
Catullo e i poeti greci (1950). See also J. Bayet, chapter on Catullus in
L'influence grecque sur la poésie latine de Catulle à Ovide, Fondation
Hardt, *Entretiens sur l'antiquité classique*, ii (1956).

22. For a recent assessment of Catullus' indebtedness to Roman tradi-
tion, see H. Bardon, 'Catulle et ses modèles poétiques de langue latine',
Latomus, 1957, 614-27.

CHAPTER II

1. This summary substantially represents, for example, the views of A. M. Duff in his article in the *Oxford Classical Dictionary* (1949), a work whose object may be taken to be the authoritative statement in brief of what is generally accepted.

2. A. L. Wheeler, *Catullus and the Traditions of Ancient Poetry* (1934), p. 62. It is only fair to state that Wheeler makes it quite clear that he is speaking of conscious allegiances, but he goes on to minimize all unconscious influences save that of the circle of Q. Lutatius Catulus and Laevius. Other writers tend to be more categorical even than Wheeler.

3. Horace, *Satires* I. 10. 17-19.

4. E.g. for Horace's opinion of the old Roman poets, see *Epistles* II. 1. 50-89.

5. See A. Rostagni, *Letteratura latina* (2nd ed., 1954), i, p. 76 ff.

6. B. A. van Groningen, *La poésie verbale grecque* (1953).

7. Ennius, *Medea*, 253-61W, and Catullus, Poem 64, opening lines.

8. As Bardon, *La littérature latine inconnue*, i (1952), p. 359, demonstrates.

9. Pliny, *Epistles* V. 3. 5-6.

10. Ibid., 2.

11. Pliny, *Epistles* IV. 14. 3.

12. We must remember, of course, we really know no more of Catullus' family connections than we do of his life. J. Suolahti, 'The Origin of the Poet Catullus', *Commentationes Linkomies* (1954), pp. 159-71, accepts tentatively the view that Catullus belonged to a branch of an old patrician family of the Verona region. We can also argue with some confidence from internal evidence pointing to the way Catullus lived and to who his associates were.

CHAPTER III

1. E. A. Havelock, *The Lyric Genius of Catullus* (1939), p. 75.

2. E.g. 'his genius [is] consistently lyrical.' (ibid., p. 85); 'Horace's odes . . . are exclusively a work of the intellect, [Catullus' lyrics] were born from the heart . . . [in Horace] only the emotion is absent. But Catullus is all emotion.' (ibid., pp. 182-3).

3. Ibid., pp. 85-6.

4. 'Catull zeigt zunächst ein doppeltes Antlitz, einmal das des von schwerer Tradition belasteten Alexandriners, dann das des urwüchsigen Naturburschen', C. *Valerius Catullus, herausgegeben und erklärt von Wilhelm Kroll* (2nd ed., 1929), Einleitung, p. vii.

5. A. M. Duff, article on Catullus in *Oxford Classical Dictionary* (1949). The epithet *doctus*, by the way, really meant 'possessing good taste'. See N. I. Herescu, *Rivista clasica*, 1930, 13-24; A. Guillemin, *R.E.L.*, 1934, 330.

6. See J. P. Elder's long and perceptive article, 'Notes on some conscious and unconscious elements in Catullus' poetry', *H.St.C.Ph.*, 1951, 101-36.

NOTES TO CHAPTER III

Cf. C. O. Brink on Poem 2 in *Latin Studies and the Humanities*, Cambridge inaugural lecture, 1956.

7. E. Diehl, *Pompeianische Wandinschriften u. Verwandtes*, Kleine Texte (1910), no. 660. Cf. no. 659.

8. J. Granarolo, 'Où en sont nos connaissances sur Catulle?', *L'information littéraire*, 1956, 59. His summing-up of Catullus' obscenity, incidentally, is excellent: 'En somme le graveleux n'est jamais chez Catulle une foi en soi (ou comme chez Rabelais une forme facile de comique), c'est plutôt une manifestation que nous pouvons regretter, mais qu'il faut définir comme telle, de son bouillant dynamisme, de sa combativité un peu fanfaronne et très ombrageuse, de sa vitalité débordante. Extrême en toute chose, impétueux de cette fougue qui se remarque chez tous les lyriques à courte vie, nous allons le voir apporter la même flamme dans ses ferveurs sentimentales, puis dans les aspirations esthétiques.'

9. *Venustus* is found six times in Catullus, but not at all in Lucretius, Virgil, Horace, Propertius or Ovid.

10. See F. O. Copley, 'Emotional conflict and its significance in the Lesbia-poems of Catullus', *A.J.Ph.*, 1949, 22-40.

11. On internal grounds only, the most likely (but quite unprovable) suggestion is that Poems 1-60 were published by Catullus, and possibly the longer poems, whereas Poems 69-116 (a much scrappier, and shorter, collection) are the work of someone who gathered together complete poems and fragments. Each poem the metre of which is not hendecasyllabic is usually followed by one or more pieces in hendecasyllabics. H. J. Mette, *Gnomon*, 1956, 34-8, proposes a much more complicated pattern, apparently assuming (wrongly) that this principle is without exception, and suggests the whole collection is modelled on an edition of Callimachus. At the very least in Poems 1-60 there can be no question of a haphazard collection of everything Catullus was known to have written. If it is the work of a later editor, he was an intelligent and sophisticated one. See A. L. Wheeler's arguments, op. cit., ch. i.

J. Granarolo, op. cit., 57-8, favours the idea of an anthology made by Catullus and later expanded. F. Della Corte, *Due studi catulliani* (1951), would make Catullus' editor Cornelius Gallus.

12. Havelock, op. cit., p. 77, on Poem 66.

13. *Idem*, on Poem 64.

14. N. I. Herescu, 'Autour de l'ironie de Catulle', *Rivista clasica*, 1941-42, 128-37.

15. See, e.g., Fr. Klingner, 'Catull', a fresh chapter added to the third edition of his *Römische Geisteswelt* (1956).

16. Kroll's note on Poem 72 is excellent: 'Lesbia hat durch eine Untreue C.s Eifersucht aufs stärkste erregt und ihn dazu veranlasst, seine Gefühle für sie zu analysieren. Er versucht, das Besondere seiner Empfindung für sie in Worte zu fassen und einer Empfindungsweise Ausdruck zu geben, die für die Antike neu war. Dabei ist völlige Klarheit nicht

erreicht und konnte nicht erreicht werden, weil die Empfindung selbst unklar war; aber das Ringen mit dem Ausdruck hat hier wie in c. 75, 76 etwas Ergreifendes. Die in Inhalt ähnliche Ausführung bei Ovid Am. 3, 11, 33 wirkt konventionell. Abgefasst ist das Gedicht nach c. 70, an das es anknüpft.' Though it is hard to reconcile this with his view of Catullus as either Alexandrian or *urwüchsiger Naturbursch.*

17. See A. L. Wheeler, 'Catullus as an elegist', *A.J.Ph.*, 1915, 173-80.

CHAPTER IV

1. The fragments of the other *poetae novi* are printed at the end of the notes to this chapter.

2. The evidence is succinctly stated by F. Della Corte, *Due studi catulliani* (1951), pp. 177-9.

3. Poem 56 is beyond doubt an extravagant fantasy. It may have been an exercise in the spirit of the Greek muse offered by a very young poet to an older one.

4. H. Bardon, *La littérature latine inconnue*, i (1952), p. 350. See Bardon for full details respecting all these persons. A more extensive account may be found in L. Alfonsi, *Poetae novi* (1945). Where a person is named in our text of Catullus, the ancient evidence about him is collected and fully discussed by C. L. Neudling, *A Prosopography to Catullus* (1955).

5. The lines addressed to Furius and Aurelius in Poem 11 are usually supposed to be ironical, but they may be a genuine appeal to friends. In Poem 23, the point of the abuse appears in the closing lines: Catullus is refusing Furius a loan. Cf. Poem 15, where lines 7-8 are a hint, perhaps, that a bond of intimacy exists, despite the abusive language. Poem 16 may be a humorously violent answer to fellow-poets who have criticized Catullus' poetry. These suggestions are not made in pursuit of a biographical will-o'-the-wisp, but because the view proposed here seriously affects our interpretation of these and other poems of Catullus.

6. Horace, *Ars poetica*, 85.

7. See B. A. van Groningen, *La poésie verbale grecque* (1953), p. 22. *Onchesmites* is unparalleled and seems deliberately formed, so that Tyrrell's comment that Cicero's words accidentally fell into hexametric form will hardly do.

8. Cicero, *Orator*, 161.

9. The final 's' is dropped seven or eight times in the *Phaenomena* which Cicero indicates (*N.D.* II. 41. 104) he wrote in early youth (*admodum adulescentulo*). The device does not occur in our fragments of the *Prognostica*, or elsewhere.

10. E.g. by C. Bione, in a vigorously and ably written article, 'Cenacoli di poeti e indirizzi culturali al tempo di Cicerone', *Mondo classico*, 1941, 156-75. H. Bardon, *R.B.Ph.*, 1948, 947-60, takes the same view.

11. The passage of Suetonius and the epigram are quoted at the end of the notes to this chapter. See N. Terzaghi, *Latomus*, 1938, 84-91.

12. See the epigrams of Furius Bibaculus, and the fragment of Cinna referring to his *Dictynna*.

13. Fondation Hardt, *Entretiens sur l'antiquité classique*, ii (1956), p. 3.

14. Cf. Fr. Klingner, *Dichter und Dichtkunst im alten Rom* (1947), p. 26: 'Es ist die mondäne Jugend der Zeit Cäsars und Ciceros, die perdita iuventus, die mit Catull in die Dichtkunst eingezogen ist.'

15. Kroll's comment on *lusi*, 'mit dichten (50, 2) hat es hier nichts zu tun', is strictly correct in that *lusi* has not here fully developed the common double meaning of living and writing about the life of wine, women and song; however, *studium* in line 18 and *studia* in line 26 stress the other side to *lusus*. Quite obviously, even if Catullus is not actually speaking of writing poetry, it is poetry he has in mind as the general context shows: Manius is the victim of unanswered love (*caelibe* in line 6 probably does not refer to actual marital status any more than words like *uir* and *coniunx* do in Roman love poetry) ; like Propertius (I. 1. 33-4) his passion will not let him sleep at night. So he has asked Catullus for a poem to console him, rather as Catullus asks Cornificius in Poem 38. [As Della Corte, *Due studi catulliani* (1951), p. 177, points out, line 3 of Poem 38 seems pretty clearly to point to a lover's unhappiness—one would not expect grief for a dead brother to go on getting worse.] Line 10 indicates that what Manius wants is a poem dealing with love, but Catullus replies excusing himself on the grounds that he no longer has heart for that sort of writing and using *lusi* to embrace both the 'iuuenum curas et libera uina' and his practice as a poet,

amores

ad caelum lepido uocare uersu.

16. 'A propos du carmen 64 de Catulle', *R.E.L.*, 1956, 190-202.

17. This emotional emptiness is well put by L. Ferrero, *Un'introduzione a Catullo* (1955), p. 25: 'Si potrà dire ancora che la tecnica era "gioco letterario", travaglio a vuoto, nei predecessori ellenistici di Catullo, mentre in questo essa fu sentita come esigenza di adeguatezza.'

18. From a poem of L. D. Lerner, 'Through Literature to Life', from *New Statesman*, 25 May 1957. I quote this poem because Mr Lerner's reaction to life and literature seems to me thoroughly Catullan.

19. 'bei Catull wird die strenge äussere Form Vehikel eines abenteuernden Geistes, der in seinen Gedichten immer neue innere Bewegungen erprobt', Fr. Klingner, *Dichter und Dichtkunst im alten Rom* (1947), pp. 26-7.

20. The way in which Propertius uses mythology 'pour l'idéalisation de Cynthie' has been well studied by P. Boyancé, Fondation Hardt, *Entretiens sur l'antiquité classique*, ii (1956), pp. 175-93. We do not in Catullus

NOTES TO CHAPTER IV

(except in Poem 68, 73-134) get this worked out at length in the poetry, but what Boyancé says of Propertius is nevertheless largely applicable.

21. In Poem 5 it gradually becomes clear that the list of kisses is deliberately phrased in a language the *senes seueriores* understand—the language of business transactions.

22. See J. P. Elder, 'Notes on some conscious and unconscious elements in Catullus' poetry', *H.St.C.Ph.*, 1951, 101-36, for a good discussion of this poem. With *furtiuus amor* cf. *furtiua munuscula*, Poem 68, 145.

23. E. A. Barber, article on 'Catullus' in *Encyclopaedia Britannica* (14th ed., 1928). Cf. 'His great virtue is sincerity', A. M. Duff in *Oxford Classical Dictionary* (1949).

24. For a fuller discussion of this point, see K. F. Quinn, 'The changing face of classical literature', *Aumla*, no. 6, 1957, 10; A. W. Allen, 'Sincerity and the Roman elegists', *C.Ph.*, 1950, 145-60.

25. See A. W. Allen, 'Elegy and the classical attitude to love', *Yale Cl.St.*, 1950, 255-77.

26. This is pointed out by E. Fraenkel, *Horace* (1957), p. 314.

27. E.g. the published discussions of metrical detail by Hopkins, Pound, or Edith Sitwell. Also Dylan Thomas's *Letters to Vernon Watkins* (1957), which may serve in many ways as a commentary on Poem 50; e.g. 'If you come to Carmarthen we could meet in the Boar's Head or somewhere and have some beer in a corner and a long lunch. . . . Bring a poem. I've just finished two poems, one over 200 lines and I'm excited about it. . . . I'll bring them both along' (p. 114).

28. 'l'imprévu des points de vue et la diversité des coloris', J. Bayet, Fondation Hardt, *Entretiens sur l'antiquité classique*, ii (1956), p. 8.

29. This question has been studied in detail by H. Bardon, *L'art de la composition chez Catulle* (1943). As examples of cyclic structure ('composition embrassée') he gives Poems 16, 33, 36, 52, 57.

30. The unsatisfactory state of our knowledge of the language of Roman poetry was deplored fifteen years ago by A. Cordier, 'La langue poétique à Rome', *Mémorial des études latines offert à J. Marouzeau* (1943), pp. 80-92. We have made little progress since.

31. One effective statement by a modern critic may be quoted: 'The poet does not have the relatively simple task (as the more naïve adherents of the doctrine of communication imply) of noting down a certain state of mind. The experience which he "communicates" is itself created by the organization of the symbols which he uses. The total poem is therefore the communication, and indistinguishable from it.' Cleanth Brooks, *Modern Poetry and the Tradition* (1939), p. 59.

32. This is the most serious fault of the translation, in many respects excellent, of Jack Lindsay. The latest translation, that of F. O. Copley (1957), appears, on the other hand, to jettison almost all the strict formal qualities of Catullus for the sake of colloquialism. The colloquialism of Catullus is strongly stressed by A. Ronconi, 'Stile e lingua di Catullo',

Atene e Roma, 1938, 139-56, in what is, to my knowledge, the only satis-
factory short overall account of Catullan language.

33. Cf. Poem 55; Horace, *Epode* 11; *Odes* I. 27, II. 4, etc.

34. Cf. Poem 10, 3; Horace *Odes* II. 11. 21.

35. For details of archaism in Catullus, see H. Heusch, *Das Archaische
in der Sprache Catulls* (1954).

36. Though note that *strophium* occurs in a seriously poetic context:
Poem 64, 65.

37. Ronconi, op. cit., p. 155.

38. Formally this is, of course, an indirect question, but here, as often,
it serves the purpose of indirect statement. The standard grammars, in-
cidentally, are curiously silent about this common usage, which occurs also
in prose, though not on the scale of the example just quoted. A most in-
teresting example is Cicero, *N.D.* I. 63: 'De diuis neque ut sint neque ut
non sint habeo dicere'—a direct translation of the Greek of Protagoras
demonstrating that Cicero was able to use *ut* to introduce indirect statement.

39. We may compare the words of Dylan Thomas: 'And I've always
disliked the weak line. I admit that readers of complicated poetry do need
a breather now and then, but I don't think the poetry should give it to them.
When they want one, they should take it and then go on.' *Letters to Vernon
Watkins* (1957), p. 29. This is quoted to show a similar attitude in a
modern poet to his work, not to imply that the poetry of Catullus is as
hard as that of Thomas, or indeed specially like it.

40. Philodemus' pronouncement that poetry, in so far as it is poetry,
does not aim at improving us (κἂν ὠφελῇ καθὸ ποίηματ' οὐκ ὠφελεῖ) is
studied by L. P. Wilkinson, 'Philodemus and Poetry', *Greece and Rome*,
1933, 144-51.

41. Horace, *A.P.* 343.

FRAGMENTS OF THE OTHER POETAE NOVI

Calvus

a uirgo infelix, herbis pasceris amaris

Bithynia quicquid
et pedicator Caesaris umquam habuit

cum grauis ingenti coniuere pupula somno

cum iam fulua cinis fuero

durum rus fugit et laboriosum.

et leges sanctas docuit et cara iugauit
corpora conubiis et magnas condidit urbes.

et talos Curius pereruditus

forsitan hoc etiam gaudeat ipsa cinis.

frigida iam celeris uergatur uistinis ora

Hesperium ante iubar quatiens

hunc tanto munere digna

Magnus, quem metuunt omnes, digito caput uno
scalpit: quid credas hunc sibi uelle? uirum.

Mens mea dira sibi praedicens omnia, uaecors

partus grauido portabat in aluo

pollentemque deum Venerem

Sardi Tigelli putidum caput uenit.

sol quoque perpetuos meminit requiescere cursus.

uaga candido
nympha quod secet ungui

Cinna

Alpinaque cummis

at nunc me Genumana per salicta
bigis raeda rapit citata nanis.

atque anquina regat stabilem fortissima cursum

atque imitata niues lucens legitur crystallus

at scelus incesto Zmyrnae crescebat in aluo.

haec tibi Arateis multum inuigilata lucernis
carmina, quis ignis nouimus aetherios,
leuis in aridulo maluae descripta libello
Prusiaca uexi munera nauicula.

lucida cum fulgent summi carchesia mali

miseras audet galeare puellas.

nec tam donorum ingenteis mirabere aceruos
innumerabilibus congestos undique saeclis,
iam inde a Belidis natalique urbis ab anno
Cecropis atque alta Tyriorum ab origine Cadmi.

saecula permaneat nostri Dictynna Catonis.

111

somniculosam ut Poenus aspidem Psyllus

te matutinus flentem conspexit Eous,
et flentem paulo uidit post Hesperus idem.

Cornificius

Centauros foedare bimembres

deducta mihi uoce garrienti

ut folia, quae frugibus arboreis tegmina gignuntur

Furius Bibaculus

Docuit multos et nobiles, uisusque est peridoneus praeceptor, maximeque
ad poeticam tendentibus, ut quidem apparere uel his uersiculis potest—
    Cato grammaticus, Latina Siren,
    qui solus legit ac facit poetas.

(Suetonius, gram. 11)

    Catonis modo, Galle, Tusculanum
    tota creditor urbe uenditabat.
    mirati sumus unicum magistrum,
    summum grammaticum, optimum poetam
    omnes soluere posse quaestiones;
    unum deficere expedire nomen.
    en cor Zenodoti, en iecur Cratetis!

confirmat dictis, simul atque exsuscitat acris
ad bellandum animos reficitque ad proelia mentes.

hic qua ducebant uastae diuortia fossae

ille graui subito deuictus uulnere habenas
misit equi lapsusque in humum defluxit et armis
reddidit aeratis sonitum.

interea Oceani linquens Aurora cubile

Iuppiter hibernas cana niue conspuit Alpes.

mitemque rigat per pectora somnum.

nam meo grabato

nomine quemque ciet: dictorum tempus adesse
commemorat.

NOTES TO CHAPTER IV

Orbilius ubinam est, litterarum obliuio?

Osce senex Catinaeque puer, Cumana meretrix

pressatur pede pes, mucro mucrone, uiro uir.

quod genus hoc hominum, Saturno sancte create?

rumoresque serunt uarios et multa requirunt.

si quis forte mei domum Catonis
depictas minio assulas et illos
custodes uidet hortuli Priapos,
miratur, quibus ille disciplinis
tantam sit patientiam adsecutus
quem tres cauliculi, selibra farris,
racemi duo tegula sub una
ad summam prope nutriant senectam.

Ticidas

felix lectule talibus
sole amoribus

Lydia doctorum maxima cura liber

CHAPTER V

1. The excesses of Tenney Frank and others are well satirized by E. A. Havelock, *The Lyric Genius of Catullus* (1939); see also R. G. C. Levens, 'Catullus', *Fifty Years of Classical Scholarship*, ed. M. Platnauer (1955).

2. From 'The truest poetry is the most feigning' in W. H. Auden, *The Shield of Achilles* (1955), p. 45.

3. This has been doubted, but it seems tolerably certain. See R. G. C. Levens, op. cit., and H. J. Mette, *Gnomon*, 1956, 34-8.

4. Lucretius IV. 1121; 1133-6. See L. Alfonsi, 'Otium e vita d'amore negli elegiaci augustei', *Studi in onore di Aristide Calderini e Roberto Paribeni* (1956), pp. 187-209. Alfonsi compares the final stanza of Poem 51.

5. Propertius II. 24. 33-8.

6. This is, e.g., the view Cicero invites his audience to form of Caelius' infatuation with Clodia. See especially *Pro Cael.* 18, 42. Caelius was probably Catullus' successor as Clodia's lover.

7. On love as the suspension of normal activities, see A. Guillemin, 'Sur les origines de l'élégie latine', *R.E.L.*, 1939, 282-92.

8. As L. Alfonsi argues, op. cit.

NOTES TO CHAPTER V

9. See E. H. Goddard, 'Propertius, Cynthia and Augustus', *C.R.*, 1923, 153-56.

10. Horace, *Satires* I. 2.

11. L. Alfonsi, op. cit., p. 187, points out that the Ciceronian discussions of *otium* in the *Pro Sestio*, etc., fall within the lifetime of Catullus.

12. Under the pressure of Augustus' campaign for social reform, poets were encouraged to express their horror of adulterous affairs, but it is obvious they were common.

13. Barber, *O.C.T.* (1953), rightly rejects the reading *nostra* in line 40, which Butler and he had adopted in their annotated edition.

14. See L. A. Post, 'Woman's place in Menander's Athens', *T.A.Ph.A.*, 1940, 420-59. The situation in Rome badly needs full investigation. See L. Alfonsi, 'L'amore-amicizia negli elegiaci latini', *Aevum*, 1945, 372-8, and idem, 'La donna nell'elegia latina,' in P. J. Enk, *Ut pictura poesis* (1955), pp. 35-44.

15. E.g. Catullus, Poems 15, 48, 56, 99; Horace, *Epodes* 11. 23; *Odes* I. 4. 19-20; III. 20; IV. 1; IV. 10; Propertius I. 20; etc.

16. See F. O. Copley, *Exclusus amator* (1955).

17. There is, of course, a greater likelihood of *actual* situations in Catullus and of literary fiction, based on *typical* situations, in Horace.

18. L. Alfonsi, 'L'amore-amicizia negli elegiaci latini', *Aevum*, 1945, 372-8, discusses the Catullan passages and traces interesting verbal parallels between the didactic writings of Cicero on friendship and the terms used by Propertius of his relationship to Cynthia. For a good study of the treatment of love as a way of life in Roman elegy see E. Burck, 'Römische Wesenszüge der Augusteischen Liebeselegie', *Hermes*, 1952, 163-200, esp. 167-82.

19. See F. O. Copley, 'Emotional conflict and its significance in the Lesbia-poems of Catullus', *A.J.Ph.*, 1949, 22-40.

20. Propertius contrasts the two ways of life in II. 23 and II. 24A; see A. W. Allen, 'Sincerity and the Roman elegists', *C.Ph.*, 1950, 145-60, on these poems.

21. See F. O. Copley, '*Seruitium amoris* in the Roman elegists', *T.A.Ph.A.*, 1947, 295-300. Whether Catullus knew the concept involves the disputed reading of Poem 68, 68.

22. E.g. E. V. Marmorale, *L'ultimo Catullo* (1952); L. Ferrero, *Un'interpretazione di Catullo* (1955). It should be remembered Poem 68 must be a fairly early poem.

CHAPTER VI

1. *C. Valerius Catullus, herausgegeben und erklärt von Wilhelm Kroll* (2nd ed., 1929), Einleitung, p. iii; cf. F. O. Copley on Poem 35, *A.J.Ph.*, 1953, 149-60.

2. See, e.g., Poem 6, last line; Poem 68, lines 45-50, and the introductory Poem 1.

3. See, e.g., the opening lines of Poems 17, 42 and 50. The straight poet-to-audience style of Poem 10 is quite exceptional.

4. T. S. Eliot, *The Three Voices of Poetry* (1953), pp. 17-18. Eliot quotes Gottfried Benn, *Probleme der Lyrik*, Vortrag in der Universität Marburg, 1951.

5. Robert Graves, *The Crowning Privilege* (1955), p. 187.

6. Kroll, commentary on Poem 8.

7. As N. I. Herescu does in an otherwise perceptive formal analysis, *R.E.L.*, 1947, 74.

8. T. S. Eliot, op. cit., pp. 5-6.

9. Also in Poem 79, and in other poems (e.g. 83), this is apparently so, though the poet does not address himself by name.

10. For a good discussion of the formal qualities and the difficulties of interpretation of this little poem, see C. O. Brink, *Latin Studies and the Humanities*, Cambridge inaugural lecture, 1956, pp. 9-13.

11. The seven Bucolics of Auden in *The Shield of Achilles* (1955) all have addressees in this Horatian sense.

12. See W. Abel, *Die Anredeformen bei den römischen Elegikern* (1930).

13. Havelock, op. cit., pp. 161-77, seems to me quite unfairly to underestimate the continuity of the Catullan movement into Augustan poetry.

Index